Kevin Liggieri

Man as Pet

.

Hermeneutics and Anthropology
Hermeneutik und Anthropologie

edited by/herausgegeben von

Prof. Dr. Andrea Marlen Esser
(Jena University)

Prof. Dr. Armin Grunwald
(Karlsruhe Institute of Technology – KIT)

Prof. Dr. Dr. Mathias Gutmann
(Karlsruhe Institute of Technology – KIT)

Volume/Band 7

LIT

Kevin Liggieri

MAN AS PET

Breeding and Optimization
in Philosophy and Literature

LIT

Cover Image: Matthias Herrgen

This book is printed on acid-free paper.

Bibliographic information published by the Deutsche Nationalbibliothek
The Deutsche Nationalbibliothek lists this publication in the Deutsche
Nationalbibliografie; detailed bibliographic data are available in the Internet at
http://dnb.dnb.de.

ISBN 978-3-643-91273-2 (pb)
ISBN 978-3-643-96273-7 (PDF)

A catalogue record for this book is available from the British Library.

© LIT VERLAG GmbH & Co. KG Wien,
Zweigniederlassung Zürich 2020
Flössergasse 10
CH-8001 Zürich
Tel. +41 (0) 76-632 84 35
E-Mail: zuerich@lit-verlag.ch   http://www.lit-verlag.ch
Distribution:
In the UK: Global Book Marketing, e-mail: mo@centralbooks.com
In North America: Independent Publishers Group, e-mail: orders@ipgbook.com
In Germany: LIT Verlag Fresnostr. 2, D-48159 Münster
Tel. +49 (0) 2 51-620 32 22, Fax +49 (0) 2 51-922 60 99, e-mail: vertrieb@lit-verlag.de

e-books are available at www.litwebshop.de

"In human beings, creature and creator are combined: in humans there is material, fragments, abundance, clay, dirt, nonsense, chaos; but in human beings there is also creator, maker, hammer-hardness, spectator-divinity and seventh day: – do you understand this contrast?"
(Friedrich Nietzsche, Beyond Good and Evil)[1]

"One can only understand the things that one tames."
(Antoine de Saint Exupéry, The Little Prince)[2]

---

[1] Friedrich Nietzsche, *Werke. Kritische Studienausgabe* (KSA). Vol 5. Ed. Giorgio Colli and Mazzino Montinari, München 1967, 161; *Beyond Good and Evil: Prelude to a Philosophy of the Future*, trans. Judith Norman, ed. Rolf-Peter Horstmann, New York 2002, 225.
[2] Antoine de Saint Exupéry, *The Little Prince* 62. https://archive.org/details/TheLittlePrince_201603, accessed 23/01/2020.

Contents

I. Anthropos and Techne

1. Anthropotechnics: A "Scandalous" Concept

On 27 September 1999, the cover of the popular German magazine *Der Spiegel* displayed the image of Arno Breker's National Socialist nude sculpture ("*Künder*") with Adolf Hitler, Lara Croft, Friedrich Nietzsche, and Superman lined up behind it (Fig. 1). This cover, and the lead story, caused a stir in the media. The title "*Gen-Projekt Übermensch. Hitler, Nietzsche, Dolly und der neue Philosophen-Streit*", announcing the twelve-page lead story, refers the reader to a "conflict of the philosophers" who were dealing with the biotechnological gene project "superman": a project supposedly situated between "Nietzsche", "Hitler", and "Dolly", the cloned sheep. If you then look at the article, you are inevitably confronted with a diverse and eye-catching array of "Visions of the Superman", from the Terminator and Superman to the androids from Fritz Lang's *Metropolis*.[3]

And among these imposing images you encounter the no less striking title in black bold letters: "*Zucht und deutsche Ordnung*": Breeding and the German Order. The subtitle provides more detailed information about the "Supermen" who seemed to be randomly arranged one after another. A key protagonist, and key terms, move into view: "With terminology like 'human breeding' and 'anthropotechnics', the philosopher Sloterdijk ignites a very German intellectual conflict. Is an era of genetically optimized human beings dawning? The transformation of the human image could change the world more than gene technology" (Fig. 2).[4]

The "Visions of the Superman" depicted on the cover and in the article thus seem to refer back to a "human breeding" or an "anthropotech-

---

[3] Marco Evers, Klaus Franke, and Johann Grolle, "Zucht und deutsche Ordnung", *Der Spiegel* 39 (1999), 300–316. This book is an extended and revised version of my piece: Kevin Liggieri, *Zur Domestikation des Menschen. Anthropotechnische und anthropoetische Optimierungsdiskurse*, Münster/Wien 2014.

[4] Ibid., 300.

Figure 1: Spiegel-Cover 39 (1999): "Gen-Projekt Übermensch. Hitler, Nietzsche, Dolly und der neue Philosophen-Streit"

Figure 2: Marco Evers, Klaus Franke, Johann Grolle, "Zucht und deutsche Ordnung", *Der Spiegel* 39 (1999), 300

nics" about which the Karlsruhe philosopher Peter Sloterdijk had kicked off a discussion. This discussion was not only conducted as a public argument between different philosophical camps, but it also flared up around the provocative concept of "anthropotechnics" itself. In the aforementioned *Spiegel* article, written by Marco Evers, Klaus Franke and Johann Grolle, the "stimulating vocabulary" of anthropotechnics, which had been brought into play by Sloterdijk only a few months previously, is interpreted as "human breeding". It was this that gave the topic a focus on (bio-)technological human modification and thus not only ignited an intellectual conflict but also, as the article itself shows, a wide-ranging media response.[5]

According to the authors of the article, Sloterdijk's term, understood along broad systematic and historical lines of discourse, successfully encompasses the most diverse possibilities for human optimization. Besides the National Socialist "Ideal Man", anthropotechnics also includes "Visions of the Super(hu)man", in-vitro fertilization, a she-goat fetus in an artificial uterus, as well as attempts at breeding and cloning generally. Questions concerning the opportunities and risks of biotechnological interventions in the human permeate the article, as well as references to Sloterdijk's problematic vocabulary of "anthropotechnics" and "human breeding", the latter of which gave rise to a "journalistic battle" between Sloterdijk's various followers and opponents (among others, Jürgen Habermas and Ernst Tugendhat).[6]

In the contemporary media and scientific landscapes, few topics generate as much controversy and are discussed with such polemic fervor as the optimization of human beings and all facets of human life. Sloterdijk's 1999 text "Rules for the Human Zoo: A Response to the Letter on Humanism" provides a good starting point for this debate. Originally delivered as a speech in Basel and Elmau, "Rules for the Human Zoo" caused uproar in the media. Another article, called "Breeder of Superhuman [*Züchter*

---

[5] Ibid., 301.

[6] See Lorenz Jäger, "Deutsches Beben. Ist die 'Kritische Theorie' am Ende? Zur Debatte um Peter Sloterdijk", *Frankfurter Allgemeine Zeitung*, 09/13/1999; Heinz-Ulrich Nennen, *Philosophie in Echtzeit. Die Sloterdijk-Debatte: Chronik einer Inszenierung. Über Metaphernfolgenabschätzung, die Kunst des Zuschauers und die Pathologie der Diskurse*, Würzburg 2003; Lars Koch, "Sloterdijk-Debatte 2.0: 'Skandalöse' Anthropologie im diskursiven Spannungsfeld von Biotechnologie, Ökonomie und Zukunftsangst", in Kristin Bulkow and Christer Petersen (Ed.), *Skandale: Strukturen und Strategien öffentlicher Aufmerksamkeitserzeugung*, Wiesbaden 2011, 87–104.

des Übermenschen]", written by Reinhard Mohr and also published in *Der Spiegel* on 6 September of the same year, was typical of the vehement attacks on Sloterdijk.[7] Mohr claimed that Sloterdijk was advocating "genetic selection" and "the leadership of a cultural elite."[8] But the claims of Mohr and other critics completely miss Sloterdijk's point, as well as the problem he was dealing with. Mohr associates the term "selection" not with a *Lektion* or an *Auslese*[9] (i.e., selection and promotion in the broadest sense, according to a set of values), but rather with the Nazi eugenics programs. Consequently, Mohr hastily concludes that "humanism is the source of the very thing that [Sloterdijk] claims to be battling." According to Mohr, Sloterdijk, "the former man of the left," has done an about face and is now trying to cause a stir with "anti-democratic, anti-Western, and even totalitarian-fascist assertions."[10] However, a closer examination shows that Sloterdijk, whose text is loaded with extremes, is not in the least concerned with *genetically* optimizing human beings, but rather with creating an open space for questions where "one has to choose a side."[11] According to Sloterdijk, it is an existential fact of human life that human beings are faced with problems "that are too difficult for them" without being afforded the luxury of "avoiding them because they are too difficult."[12] The scientist Julian Huxley, brother of the author Aldous Huxley (*Brave New World*), coined the concepts "evolutionary humanism" and "transhumanism" precisely in the context of such problems. Both of these concepts refer to the fact that man can and must steer his own development: "I believe in transhumanism: once there are enough people who can truly say that, the human species will be on the threshold of a new kind of existence, as different from ours as ours is from that of Peking man. It will at last be

---

[7] Reinhard Mohr, "Züchter des Übermenschen", *Der Spiegel* 36 (1999), 268–271; Mohr, "Der Herr Blasen", *Der Spiegel* 52 (2002), 156–157.

[8] Ibid., 270. For more on the conflict, see Sjoerd von Tuinen, *Peter Sloterdijk. Ein Profil*, 2. Ed., Paderborn 2007, 125–149.

[9] Peter Sloterdijk, *Regeln für den Menschenpark. Ein Antwortschreiben zu Heideggers Brief über den Humanismus*, Frankfurt a. M. 1999, 43.

[10] Mohr, "Züchter des Übermenschen", 270.

[11] Peter Sloterdijk in an interview. Cf. Sabine Schmidt and Peter Sloterdijk, "Anthropotechnik: Der Mensch gestaltet sich selbst", *Das Magazin*, 11 (2000), 10.

[12] Sloterdijk, *Menschenpark*, 47; "Rules for the Human Zoo: a response to the Letter on Humanism", *Environment and Planning D: Society and Space* 27 (2009), 12–28, p. 24. In cases where the English translation did not contain all the original sentences, the German edition was used.

consciously fulfilling its real destiny."[13] Huxley, like other researchers,[14] saw a new phase of evolution as opening up, a revolution in evolution that man must take into his own hands. This challenge is analogous to the problematic raised in Sloterdijk's text.

Turning now from media criticism to the central theme of "Human Zoo", it becomes clear that, within the domain of the cultural sciences, Sloterdijk is reviving a concept that is still regarded as problematic today. It is the concept of "anthropotechnics." The significance of this concept for Sloterdijk lies in the notion of the self-application of technologies to man. If the media is to be believed, Sloterdijk's concept of "anthropotechnics" "provokes" an "incredible disgust."[15] But when the etymological composition of the term is examined more closely, it can easily be seen that it is made up of the word 'anthropos' (ἄνθρωπος), which can be translated as 'man', and 'techne' (τέχνη). This latter Greek term already gives pause for thought, because it has little in common with the modern conception of a purely mechanical technology. "The ancient Greek word *techne* corresponds more readily to the concept of design than it does to our everyday understanding of technology. It also concerns art and the artificial, forms and the act of formation."[16] In antiquity *techne* meant an art in service of life (skill as well as ingenuity) that combines in itself knowledge and science. *Anthropo-techne* would accordingly be the art and the craft of forming human beings, a process that also encompasses *poeisis*. The socialized human being is already the product of an anthropotechnics and is a success story in the domain of optimization. It is precisely because man is not a purely natural being that the process by which he becomes man implies *techne*. It might even be said that the hominid has completed the process of becoming man and is therefore already post- or transhuman.[17]

---

[13] Julian Huxley, "Transhumanism", in Huxley (Ed.), *New Bottles for New Wine. Essays*, London 1957, 13–17, p. 17.

[14] Christina Brandt, "Die Diffusion des zukünftigen Menschen: Klonpraktiken und Visionen des Humanen, 1960–1980", in Florenze Vienne and Christina Brandt (Ed.), *Wissensobjekt Mensch. Humanwissenschaftliche Praktiken im 20. Jahrhundert*, Berlin 2008, 213–243, p. 226.

[15] *Spiegel* 39 (1999), 300.

[16] Norbert Bolz, *Das Gestell*, Paderborn 2012, 100.

[17] Ibid., 105. We will return to the notion of a self-formation (technology of the self) as an artwork in which *aesthesis* and *poeisis* are combined in the literary portion of this study, which deals with 'anthropoetics'. Conceptually, anthropo-*technics* and anthro-*poetics* can be read together.

According to the philosophical anthropologist Helmuth Plessner, man is by nature "half-way" and from his very origins he has had to discover an "artificiality" in order "to come into balance with himself and the world."[18]

Sloterdijk is not the founder of the concept of anthropotechnics. When this concept is considered genealogically, we see that it had already appeared in France at the start of the 19th century and then made its way, through various transnational translations, into the *Great Soviet Encyclopedia* of 1926, where the term designated the possibility, speculatively anticipated, of biotechnologically manipulating human genetic material.[19] This encyclopedia defines "anthropotechnics" as "an applied branch of biology that tasks itself with improving the physical and mental characteristics of human beings using the same methods that zootechnics does to improve and cultivate new breeds of domesticated animals."[20] By this definition, anthropotechnics is modelled after animal and plant husbandry, i.e., "zootechnics."[21] One recurring motif – and a motif that already appears among the concept's fundamental features – is that of *domestication*. This word has a twofold meaning that is central to our considerations here. Domestication is at once the *taming* of wild animals, that is, domesticating them, as well as the *breeding* of these animals (in a third sense it also refers to the cultivation of wild-growing plants).[22] Thus, in 1954, the zoologist Konrad Lorenz recognized that "the domestication of specific kinds of animals [...] is humanity's oldest biological experiment."[23]

---

[18] Helmuth Plessner, *Die Stufen des Organischen und der Mensch. Einleitung in die philosophische Anthropologie* (1928), Berlin/New York 1975, 321. See further Julia Gruevska, "Kultur als 'ontische Notwendigkeit': Wilhelm Diltheys und Helmuth Plessners psychophysische Auffassung des Lebens", in Ralf Glitza and Kevin Liggieri (Ed.), *Kultur und Bildung. Die Geisteswissenschaften und der Zeitgeist des Naturalismus*, Freiburg i. Br. 2019, 52–66.

[19] Kevin Liggieri, *"Anthropotechnik". Zur Geschichte eines umstrittenen Begriffs*, Göttingen 2020.

[20] *Great Soviet Encyclopedia*, 65 vols. and one supplementary volume. 1st Ed. Moscow 1926–1933, ed. by Soviet Encylopedia, LLC., Vol. 3, 130–131. I am grateful to Michael Hagemeister for this translation.

[21] Cf. Alexander Etkind, *Eros Of The Impossible: The History Of Psychoanalysis In Russia*, trans. Noah & Maria Rubins, Boulder 1997, 330.

[22] Cf. Hans-Jörg Rheinberger and Staffan Müller-Wille, *A Cultural History of Heredity*, Chicago 2012.

[23] Konrad Lorenz, "Psychologie und Stammesgeschichte" (1954), in Konrad Lorenz, *Über tierisches und menschliches Verhalten. Aus dem Werdegang der Verhaltenslehre*, München 1965, Vol. 2, 201–255, p. 239.

Accord to Lorenz, man and cave dwelling bears are the only living beings who have ever "domesticated themselves."[24] For zoologists, this "self-domestication" is the single decisive enabling condition for man's becoming human.[25]

This taming process was already underway in human prehistory. 40,000 years ago, man trained the wolf to be his companion.[26] Prehistoric men lived with tamed wolves and killed or drove off the wilder ones, so that only the harmless ones were able to reproduce. They were already unwittingly applying the principle of selection. During this long period of coexistence (ca. 20,000 years), the bones and the structure of those tamed animals began to change. The result was our pet, the dog. The dog-man connection can thus be seen as the first success story in taming and domestication.[27] All breeding began with domestication. Man experimented with great enthusiasm in horticulture too. Over the generations, men have bred their crops and their pets to such an extent that they are now far from their biological origins and some hardly resemble to their wild relatives and would not be able to survive without human intervention.

When dealing with plants and animals, the breeder selects those individuals from the stock that best represent the trait he wants to foster. The particular features of what I will call the *anthropotechnical triangle* (taming, breeding, and training/education) will become increasingly visible over the course of this work. There are two conceptions of "technics" that underlie my investigation of these three concepts. The first is of "technics" as a specialized ability, a technology, a practice of knowledge, a *techne* of intervention. From antiquity onward, $τέχνη$ in this sense designates a "goal-oriented and appropriate" art (skill or dexterity) that comprises knowledge as well as science.[28] The second sense is that of "technics" as a concrete technology and a technology of production that uses various biotechnolo-

---

[24] Ibid., 240.

[25] Ibid., 241, 243.

[26] Juliet Clutton-Brock, *A Natural History of Domesticated Mammals*, New York 1999; Pam J. Crabtree, Douglas V. Campana, Kathleen Ryan (Ed.), *Early Animal Domestication and Its Cultural Context*, Philadelphia 1989.

[27] James Serpell (Ed.), *The Domestic Dog: Its Evolution, Behaviour and Interactions with People*, New York 2002.

[28] "Technik", in *Historisches Wörterbuch der Philosophie*, ed. Joachim Ritter and Karlfried Gründer, Vol. 10, Basel 1998, 940–952, p. 940. On the complex concept of $τέχνη$, see the comprehensive publication of Rudolf Löbl, *Texnh–Techne. Untersuchungen zur Bedeutung dieses Worts in der Zeit von Homer bis Aristoteles*, Vol. 1: *Von Homer bis*

gies to form the body, attaching prostheses to it in order to optimize it. Both meanings of "technics" are, of course, closely connected.

It can also be noted that cybernetic concepts are frequently inscribed into the cultural-scientific notion of these anthropotechnics.[29] Accordingly, Sloterdijk identifies cybernetics (a technological science of control) as *the* defining characteristic of modernity. He connects optimization with cybernetics and sees a new compromise emerging between individualism and cybernetics, a mechanical ontology that unleashes new understandings of self-development and self-cultivation [*Bildung*].[30] He believes that "one must become a cyberneticist in order to remain a humanist."[31] Semantic transformation is a significant part of this new mode of thinking, because, as the media philosopher Erich Hörl points out, the technological displacement of meaning creates completely new cultures of signification. Through the destruction of traditional "significant and hermeneutic" sense-content and its replacement by sense-content created by technology, what is called "meaning" becomes likewise reorganized and reoriented.[32] According to Sloterdijk's diagnosis, a post-semantism develops alongside posthumanism. It will become clear over the course of this work that, and how, meaning and being are often thought together in closely related conceptual networks, and how deconstructive the effect of modern optimization technologies will be on these networks.

---

zu den Sophisten, Würzburg 1997, Vol. 2: *Von den Sophisten bis Aristoteles*, Würzburg 2003.

[29] Sloterdijk, *Du musst dein Leben ändern*, Frankfurt a. M. 2009, 23; *You must change your life*, trans. Wieland Hoban, New York 2013, 1–19. In cases where the English translation did not contain all the original sentences, the German edition was used. The concept 'cybernetics' will be applied in the following to describe mechanical and self-regulating processes. Cybernetics is a science of control ("the art of control") that observes how processes react on machines and how these control themselves. In modern discourse, cybernetics is increasingly regarded as "ontological and epistemological, a formation crucial to the history of power, as well as subjectivity and desire." With cybernetics we are entering the field of a "post-significant order of meaning." (Erich Hörl, "Die Technologische Bedingung. Zur Einführung", in Erich Hörl (Ed.), *Die technologische Bedingung*. Frankfurt a. M. 2011, 7–53, p. 10). For Hörl, cybernetic relations are determined by the fact that they describe meanings and objects that are in turn "systematic, active, intelligent, and capable of communication." (Ibid., 25)

[30] Sloterdijk, "Optimierung des Menschen?", https://www.youtube.com/watch?v=4cBXJEwsjUM, min. 42:00, accessed 01/23/2020.

[31] Ibid. It is precisely from this "non-humanity" that Sloterdijk sees great opportunities arising for man. (cf. Tuinen, *Sloterdijk*, 111)

[32] Hörl, "Die technologische Bedingung", 11.

Because of its relevance to the cultural sciences, I will primarily use Sloterdijk's concept of anthropotechnics throughout this investigation. Nonetheless, I will use the concept in a more specific sense than its broader applications. The concept's peripheral uses will be unified into a single genetic, as well as eugenic, discourse that is itself located within the framework of a biotechnological optimization of man from the inside out. By "inside", I mean an intervention "into" man, that is, into his physically existing body.

What, according to Sloterdijk, is anthropotechnics? It is the transformation of the natural into the artificial, a process that man applies to himself. As I have already mentioned, "technics" is to be understood in the classical sense of *techne*, a methodical process, a skill by means of which one attains certain goals. Anthropotechnics proceeds from the assumption that there is no such thing as a permanently fixed human nature that serves as the measure of man. Sloterdijk is less concerned with thematizing the point of intersection *between* man and machine than he is with taking on the task of "optimizing" man – a process of optimization that, as most of Sloterdijk's critics fail to see, has nothing to do with eugenics, cloning, or the human genome project.[33] Rather, Sloterdijk reflects on what is at stake when human beings labor on human beings.[34] What happens when man himself becomes an object to be modified? The most extreme conceivable position for Sloterdijk is one in which anthropotechnics becomes a "God-technology" in which "man plays God."[35] Sloterdijk advances the thesis that man has the ability to create himself.[36] He is an auto-demiurge. What is most important here is that Sloterdijk does not see this demiurgical capacity as lying in genetic technology, but rather in 18th-century educational programs. "Self-cultivation [*Bildung*] is the typical modern humanistic desire to make man into a book that speaks about his own experience of the world."[37] By framing anthropotechnics as a transtemporal concept, Sloterdijk lays out three concepts of self-care, which will be examined over the course of this analysis. In addition to genetic technology and education, he

---

[33] Cf. Mohr, "Züchter des Übermenschen", 268–271.

[34] Sloterdijk, "Optimierung des Menschen?", min. 18:30.

[35] Ibid., min. 22:25.

[36] See also Joshua Lederberg, "Die biologische Zukunft des Menschen", in Robert Jungk and Hans-Josef Mundt (Ed.), *Das umstrittene Experiment: Der Mensch*, München 1966, 292–301, p. 298.

[37] Sloterdijk, "Optimierung des Menschen?", min. 30:00.

also includes the notions of *prosthesis* (prosthetic limbs, mechanical supplementation), *athletics* (physical training and discipline), and *cosmetics* (any enhancement in the broadest sense of the term). All three realms of anthropotechnics connect "the care of the self" to the work performed by human beings in order to optimize themselves.[38]

Sloterdijk's notion of anthropotechnics can therefore be understood in a broad sense as covering many interdisciplinary realms. However, in the ten years between *The Human Zoo* (1999) and his comprehensive book *You Must Change your Life* (2009), Sloterdijk shifts the emphasis in his use of this concept. Whereas in *The Human Zoo* he was primarily concerned with the "entanglement of taming and breeding",[39] ten years later he is more interested in systems of training. "[A]ll the forms of self-referential practising and working on one's own vital form. [...] I bring together in the term 'anthropotechnics'."[40] Anthropotechnics is defined as "the mental and physical forms of exercise with which men of various cultures have endeavored to optimize their cosmic and social immune status in the face of vague risks of life and acute certainties of death."[41]

Sloterdijk's gambit here tactically forestalls any debate about eugenics, since the very notion of training rules out a genetic program. Training is rather defined as repetition in the service of bodily and spiritual improvement.[42] Training is not a radical, external intervention into the human, nor does it involve stigmatized concepts like "selection". Despite this shift in emphasis, Sloterdijk is still preoccupied with the fact that anthropotechnics is directed toward human beings. Human beings have no choice but to produce themselves. That is the meaning of the concept of anthropotechnics. Human beings live in fields of activity, of which they themselves are the results. We are condemned to the task of forming ourselves. Consequently, man is driven vertically – he can make more or less of himself.[43] According to Sloterdijk, man therefore possesses a responsibility for self-

---

[38] Ibid., min. 32:00.

[39] Sloterdijk, *Menschenpark*, 41; *The Human Zoo*, 23, translation modified.

[40] Sloterdijk, *Du musst dein Leben ändern*, 8.

[41] Sloterdijk, "Die Revolution der gebenden Hand", *Frankfurter Allgemeine Zeitung* 23 (2009), 23, quoted from Willem Schinkel and Liesbeth Noordegraaf-Eelens, "Peter Sloterdijk's Spherological Acrobatics: An Exercise in Introduction", in Willem Schinkel and Liesbeth Noordegraaf-Eelens (Ed.), *In Medias Res: Peter Sloterdijk's Spherological Poetics of Being*, Amsterdam 2011, 7–28, p. 19.

[42] Ibid., 14.

[43] Sloterdijk, *Du musst dein Leben ändern*, 245, 515.

formation that he cannot simply hand over to a higher authority. "The idea that the world will somehow do it for us has a fatal, fatalistic aspect to it."[44] Man has to formulate "a codex of anthropotechnics and to confront this fact actively."[45] Criticism of technology becomes groundless in the truest sense of the word: it lacks any ground so long as technology is part of our daily reality, a part that cannot simply be thought away. When the medium has become our environment, the question of whether the medium is good or evil can no longer be answered. Using the medium of "technology," man can set completely new limits to his being, or so many natural scientists and sociologists believe. The "determining factors of man's being are being overtaken and over-stepped, all at once," says the historian of science Christina Brandt. By the same token, "the human body of the future [...] from its inside out is being thought as plastic and subject to a potentially infinite number of transformations."[46] It follows that we can no longer speak of "the limits of our bodies, but rather the limits of my devices [...], the limits of my world."[47] Given this biotechnological way of looking at modernity, anthropotechnics in its strong sense seems to be a 20th-century phenomenon. As against this prejudice, Sloterdijk shows that anthropotechnics is not a modern invention, but rather one that had already appeared in antiquity and, above all, in humanism. "Such a codex [of anthropotechnics, K.L.] will retroactively alter the meaning of the old humanism, for it will make explicit, and codified, that humanity is not just the friendship of man with man, but that man has become the higher power for man."[48]

It can be extrapolated from Sloterdijk's thesis, at least to a certain extent and in relation to the cultural-scientific application of anthropotechnics, that not only genetic interventions, but all processes of "formation," of self-cultivation, educating, socializing, and civilizing human beings can be regarded as anthropotechnics. Even if too much is sometimes attributed to the term, Sloterdijk's initial position, namely, that man must form himself, select himself, and relate to himself can nonetheless be grasped in a tech-

---

44 Paul Vogler, "Disziplinärer Methodenkontext und Menschenbild", in Hans Georg Gadamer and Paul Vogler (Ed.), *Neue Anthropologie*, München 1972, Vol. 1. *Biologische Anthropologie*, 3–22, p. 11.

45 Sloterdijk, *Menschenpark*, 45; *The Human Zoo*, 24.

46 Brandt, "Die Diffusion des zukünftigen Menschen", 219.

47 Bolz, *Das Gestell*, 105.

48 Sloterdijk, *Menschenpark*, 45; *The Human Zoo*, 24.

nological manner, namely, as how he forms himself and intervenes in his own being. Anthropotechnics "functions as the theorem of an 'historical anthropology' according to which the human condition is fundamentally a product and can only be understood by analyzing its historically varying modes and relations of production. Anthropotechnics in this sense must be understood as a new configuration of ontology and anthropology beyond Heidegger's critical opposition of technology and poetry."[49]

It would seem to be a matter of indifference here whether one calls anthropotechnics pedagogy, birth politics, genetic engineering, or enhancement. The broader definition of anthropotechnics can be succinctly and schematically expressed as consisting of the aforementioned tricolon: *breeding*, *taming*, and *education/training*. I will examine this anthropotechnical triangle more closely in the following.

2. Between Pet and God

Since the advent of the modern era, anthropotechnics has been conceived of, on the one hand, as technologies of improvement. The assumption underlying this conception is that human beings, as they are, have failed, are deficient, or are, at the very least, capable of being improved. On the other hand, the concept of breeding is relatively recent and it is very closely connected to the definition of "life" advanced by the natural sciences (population statistics, modern evolutionary theory, hereditary biology, and genetics).[50] As the instrumentalization of life (*bios*) in modernity has increasingly moved to the center of scientific considerations, its science, namely biology, has gradually become the master discipline. "Now life stands at the center, not man, and the discipline that devotes itself to the solution

---

[49] Sjoerd van Tuinen, "'Transgenous Philosophy': Posthumanism, Anthropotechnics and the Poetics of Natal Difference", in Schinkel and Noordegraaf-Eelens (Ed.), *In Medias Res*, 43–66, p. 55.

[50] Cf. Petra Gehring, "Zwischen Menschenpark und Soft Eugenics", in Petra Gehring. (Ed.), *Was ist Biomacht? Vom zweifelhaften Mehrwert des Lebens*, Frankfurt a. M. 2006, 154–184, p. 154. This meaning can of course be retroactively applied to the concept of 'breeding'. On the notion of breeding (especially that of animals) since the early modern era see Hans-Jörg Rheinberger and Staffan Müller–Wille (Ed.), *Heredity Produced: At the Crossroads of Biology, Politics and Culture, 1500–1870*, New York 2007.

of this problem is called biology, not anthropology."[51] In *The Human Zoo* Sloterdijk also comes to the conclusion that power is being applied to life more and more directly.[52] "Life" thus designates "the privileged terrain on which measures of control and guidance operate."[53] In 1968, Theo Löbsack had noted the emphasis that has been set on biology as it relates to man. He presciently remarked that "biology [...] will influence our lives in a more lasting way in the foreseeable future than nuclear power has been able to."[54] It is the discipline that can "intervene in the balance of nature, as well as in the processes of life itself, to heal as well as to destroy."[55] The historian of science Georges Canguilhem accurately describes biology as "one of the ways by which humanity seeks to take control of its destiny and to transform its being into a duty. For this project, man's knowledge about man is of fundamental importance. The primacy of anthropology is not a form of anthropomorphism, but a condition for anthropogenesis."[56] Has the search for man's unchangeable "essence" therefore lost its significance with the rise of biology and its attendant technologies? Or is it perhaps that we have discovered something that we did not want to discover? An emptiness? The birth of scientific biology around 1800 brought about an epistemological rupture, because then man, and life itself, became the focus of scientific research. It can be asked whether it is man's nature to have no nature.[57] Michel Foucault makes a similar argument when he says that "nothing in man – not even his body – is sufficiently stable to serve as the

---

[51] Wolf Lepenies, "Naturgeschichte und Anthropologie im 18. Jahrhundert", in Bernhard Fabian, Wilhelm Schmidt-Biggemann and Rudolf Vierhaus (Ed.), *Deutschlands kulturelle Entfaltung – Die Neubestimmung des Menschen*, München 1980, 211–226, p. 222.

[52] Cf. Tuinen, *Sloterdijk*, 103–113.

[53] Ulrich Bröckling and Matthias Schöning, *Disziplinen des Lebens? Zwischen Anthropologie, Literatur und Politik*, Tübingen 2004, 11.

[54] Theo Löbsack, *Die Biologie und der liebe Gott. Aspekte einer zukunftsreichen Wissenschaft*, München 1968, 13.

[55] Wolfgang Wieser, Einleitung. "Das umstrittene Experiment: Der Mensch – Grenzen und Möglichkeiten wissenschaftlicher Prognosen", in Robert Jung and Hans Josef Mundt (Ed.), *Das umstrittene Experiment: Der Mensch*, München 1966, 9–10.

[56] Georges Canguilhem, *Knowledge of Life*, trans. Stefanos Geroulanos and Daniela Ginsburg, New York 2008, 19.

[57] The anthropological *essentia* is to be understood in this context as an unchangeable characteristic of man.

basis for self-recognition or for understanding other men."[58] A tendency emerges with scientific biology that must be examined more closely.

Modern man is "a man without qualities" in the truest sense. A freedom and an obligation are disclosed to him. This "creature of defects" (Mängelwesen) 'man', must, on the one hand, define himself and he can, at the same time, transform himself into something more. Lack, as an "identifying feature of degeneration", is a central reference point here.[59] The deficiency that is the fate of human beings always brings with it the possibility of taking action against this deficiency. Hence failure can be understood as opportunity. With his programmatic diagnosis of "the disappearance of man"[60], Foucault follows Nietzsche who had seen the *Übermensch* as a possibility beyond man that is to be thought. Thus man is only an actor who has no sooner stepped on the epistemic stage than he disappears from it once more, "like a face drawn in the sand by edge of the sea."[61] Following Foucault, we can conclude that we are at some distance from traditional humanism: we have left the old and familiar image of man behind. Transhumanism appears when the human is in the process of dissolving and man becomes an experiment. Man's physical body is of ever greater significance to this discourse as it fits into an instrumental, experimental setting. "The 'experiment' of 'humanity', that is, man's manipulation of himself, has begun – is even in full swing. This experiment has opened the way to a radical new epoch in human history. Research now strives to penetrate into the fabric of man and of humanity, to give it new form, to deconstruct man as we know him today in this way and, one might say, to put an entirely new being in his place." [62] Although, in this quotation from his 1967 book *Experiment Humanity*, Paul Overhage is primarily referring to the debate about genetics, he nonetheless addresses a discourse – that of the optimization of "the new man" – whose conceptual roots are far older.

---

[58] Michael Foucault, "Nietzsche, Genealogy, History", in Foucault, *Language, Counter-Memory, Practice: Selected Essays and Interviews*, ed. Donald F. Bouchard, Ithaca 1977, 139–164, p. 153.

[59] Heiko Stoff, "Eine Geschichte der Dinge und eine dingliche Geschichte des Menschen. Methodische Probleme", in Brandt and Vienne (Ed.), *Wissensobjekt Mensch. Humanwissenschaftliche Praktiken im 20. Jahrhundert*, 43–67, p. 60.

[60] Michel Foucault, *The Order of Things. An Archaeology of the Human Sciences*, London/New York 2004, 421.

[61] Ibid., 422.

[62] Paul Overhage, *Experiment Menschheit. Die Steuerung der menschlichen Evolution*, Frankfurt a. M. 1967, 6.

His statement can be brought into relation to the experiments in humanity of the early modern period or of the 18th century. Man has always been the starting point as well as the goal of these experiments.[63]

The present study will cover the programmatic texts of Tommaso Campanella (Breeding I), Immanuel Kant (Education a), Wilhelm von Humboldt (Education b), and Ellen Key (Breeding II), as well as the literature of human optimization present in texts by Johann Wolfgang von Goethe, Heinrich von Kleist, and Friedrich Hölderlin. These texts can offer outlooks as well as insights. They are variable as well as exemplary in this respect, because the central concepts of anthropotechnics could have been elucidated by drawing on Plato, Friedrich Schiller, or Friedrich Nietzsche.[64] We will be covering a period of nearly 500 years with the texts selected and – in full awareness of the attendant methodological dangers – will make huge leaps across the historical timeline. Nonetheless historical causality is so complex that, although Key and Humboldt stand in a much closer temporal proximity, her 1900 project has much more in common with Campanella's project from around the turn of the 17th century. That there are breaks and epistemic paradigm shifts is indisputable. Nonetheless, one cannot speak of a "progress" that is unidirectional. Rather, anthropotechnics seems to be arranged around a pool of ideas. Diverse patterns that emerge frequently are then worked out over the course of centuries: the politics of birth, the education of children, the education of educators, the forming of plans and collectives, technologies of the self, and the hope for a better future, a better humanity, a better race. When considering the subject of historical difference, it can be noted that large portions of the concept of anthropotechnics are associated with "peoples" or "races" well into the middle of the 20th century.[65] A present or future collective must always be transformed into its optimal form. Accordingly, earlier attempts at breeding were social interventions. That is particularly evident in Campanella's work: he has no interest in directly modifying man's biological nature. This tradition consists of cultural interventions

---

[63] Naturally, it is an accepted view that experiments and the knowledge that they produce can be changed and modified.

[64] Plato and Nietzsche are treated as anthropotechnicians by Sloterdijk: see Sloterdijk, *Menschenpark*, 37–45 (Nietzsche) and 47–54 (Plato).

[65] Cf. Staffan Müller-Wille and Christina Brandt (Ed.), *Heredity Explored: Between Public Domain and Experimental Science, 1850–1930*, Cambridge 2016.

into procreative behavior (as promoted by Key and Campanella), but not of direct intervention into "the cellular dimension of procreation itself."[66]

In the 1950s and 1960s, however, new possibilities in medical research made invasive interventions into the human body possible. Hence "the artificial breeding of human beings" became "an attainable research goal."[67] The goal of such research was to produce "a lost genetic balance not through marriage laws, sterilization measures, or even through the eradication of human beings, that is, from the outside, but rather from the inside, through physical or chemical manipulation of the embryo."[68] The change that took place within genetic discourse was that it no longer concerned the simple intervention *into* the body – that was already the desired goal of birth politics – but rather changing or improving individuals through science or technology. From the still-distant cloning of human beings all the way down to everyday genetic enhancements, the new anthropotechnics focuses on aspects of the individual instead of wanting to transform society as a whole.[69] This personal-genetic anthropotechnics as a kind of enhancement enriches the individual; although the individual is now defined as the sum of his genes. What one produces over the course of one's life and what one hands over to the political regime is the genotype itself. "The politics of breeding no longer applies to 'someone'. The person is cancelled out."[70] To simply see the previous goals of optimization as removed from the genetic discourse would be one-sided, because traditional anthropotechnics – i.e., of the school, the military, the prison, in short, socialization its entirety – runs parallel to this discourse. It is a medical and social illusion to think that anthropotechnics has only been applied in eugenics or in 20th-century genetic research, even if these intellectual currents made it more acute and gave it a praxis.[71]

---

[66] Brandt, "Die Diffusion des zukünftigen Menschen", 218.

[67] Friedrich Wagner, "Die Manipulierung des Menschen durch Genwissenschaft. Geschichte, Methoden, Ziele und Folgen", in Wagner (Ed.), *Menschenzüchtung. Das Problem der genetischen Manipulation des Menschen*, München 1969, 13–49, p. 15.

[68] Ibid.

[69] Cf. Alison Bashford and Philippa Levine (Ed.), *The Oxford Handbook of the History of Eugenics*, New York 2010.

[70] Gehring, "Zwischen Menschenpark und Soft Eugenics", 175.

[71] Cf. Kevin Liggieri, "'[A]n der Front des Kampfes um den Menschen selbst'. Anthropogenetik und Anthropotechnik im sowjetischen Diskurs der 1920er Jahre", in *Berichte zur Wissenschaftsgeschichte* 2 (2016), 165–184.

It is for these reasons that the first part of this book will focus on traditional texts that take philosophical, sociological-pedagogical anthropotechnics as their theme. The objection that a modern perspective is taken in this study that applies the concept of anthropotechnics to historical texts can only be avoided by letting the texts speak for themselves, and by thereby demonstrating that "modern" anthropotechnics is substantively indebted to the methods and ideas of texts from the 1600s, 1800s, and 1900s.

The first, cultural-historical part of this work will lay the groundwork for the second by considering *breeding* (in Campanella and Key) and *education* (in Kant and Humboldt). Nonetheless, it would be incorrect to conclude that the notion of taming will be left out of this analysis. We might think of taming as a goal towards which the other two concepts are moving. It is in this sense that Nietzsche can – not without justification – ridicule this domestication of human beings when he writes: "Virtue is whatever makes modest and tame; this is how they made the wolf into a dog and mankind himself into mankind's favorite pet."[72] A postulate common to the various anthropotechnics is that one must be "better," "more human," "better adjusted" – although for the most part this simply means "tamer", better socialized.

This book is divided schematically into a historical section and a systematic section. The former also serves as a prolegomenon to the latter. It focuses on various aspects of anthropotechnics (breeding, education, taming). The historical portion must inevitably raise the question of the historicity of anthropotechnics, even though it is not my intention to write the history of this term here.[73] Rather, I wish to provide an overview of the historical development of anthropotechnical discourse, with an eye towards the historical situation in which it was created. This study is not, however, an analysis of historical events, but rather an analysis of the history of a discourse. Accordingly, the first part is devoted to breeding, since it is here

---

[72] Nietzsche, KSA 4, 214, *Thus Spoke Zarathustra*, trans. Adrian Del Caro and Robert Pippin, New York 2006, 135. What is usually counted as positive in the process of socialization is seen by Nietzsche as a technique that weakens strength. Like Nietzsche, Sloterdijk also questions the "breeding monopoly" (Sloterdijk, *Menschenpark*, 42; *The Human Zoo*, 22). Sloterdijk nonetheless recognizes that there is no sovereign as far as breeding is concerned. There is "breeding without a breeder" and thus an "agentless biocultural drift" (ibid.; *The Human Zoo*, 23).

[73] Cf. Liggieri, *"Anthropotechnik". Zur Geschichte eines umstrittenen Begriffs*, Göttingen 2020.

that birth politics aims to modify the heredity factors themselves and it is here that the hygienic treatment of biological materials is foregrounded, together with education, in latter of which, by contrast, it is consciousness that is acted upon. An anthropology develops pragmatically within education, specifically in relation to cognitive development. This emphasis on the applied aspects of the problematic of schooling and education in Kant and Humboldt can be understood as a pedagogical anthropotechnics, since it is precisely pedagogy that, according to Sloterdijk, "sharp-wittedly rose to become the discipline of all disciplines. It single-mindedly combined the crude education-political imperative – supplying the modern state with usable human beings – with a modern form of the absolute imperative: 'Instead of changing your life later on, you should let us change you from the start.'"[74]

Society attempts to set the supreme "imperative of humanization" within the framework of institutional education.[75] But because this optimization no longer concerns just an elite, but instead a mass of human beings, the educational system requires the institution of the "school". The belief that "he who has the children, has the future" is not only one that is embraced by totalitarian governments, but also by humanistic thinkers like Kant and Humboldt.

In the second part of this book, after historically setting the epistemic tableau and laying out the central parameters in prescriptive texts and performative examples, I will examine the optimization discourse in literature.

Accordingly, we have to ask: "What defines an *anthro-poetics* as an anthropotechnical literature?" To answer this question, I will proceed from the assumption that literature observes processes of anthropotechnics in political, economic, and educational systems and integrates them into its own system. Naturally, literature does not do so by using the scientific coding of true and false, but rather with its own particular system of coding, namely, boring and interesting. Hence the presence of cyborgs, artificial human beings, and new "supermen" in the literary repertoire evokes excitement.[76] The optimization of human beings in literature (*anthropoetics*) is a success as regards communication, because the material has been updated

---

[74] Sloterdijk, *Du musst dein Leben ändern*, 545; *You must change your life*, 346.

[75] Ibid., 548; *You must change your life*, 348.

[76] We prefer to use Niklas Luhmann's sociological system theory, from which we have taken this terminology. (Cf. Niklas Luhmann, *Schriften zur Kunst und Literatur*, ed. Niels Werber, Frankfurt a. M. 2008.)

again and again. I will select certain exemplary literary works in order to demonstrate how an anthropotechnics has been inscribed in them.

The fundamental concern of this analysis, which is sometimes subtle, sometimes quite prominent in both the philosophico-historical and the literary portions, is to show the relevance of anthropotechnics and anthropoetics. To this end, the analysis, like that of Foucault, does not write "the history of solutions" but rather undertakes "the genealogy of problems, of *problèmatiques*."[77] It is in this vein that Sloterdijk can emphatically state: "[...] the discourse about the difference and the entanglement of taming and breeding – indeed [...] intimations of anthropotechnics in general – these are prospects from which we may not, in the present day, avert our eyes."[78]

---

[77] Michel Foucault, "On the genealogy of ethics: an overview of work in progress", in Paul Rabinow (Ed.), *The Foucault Reader*, New York 1984, 343.
[78] Sloterdijk, *Menschenpark*, 41ff,; *The Human Zoo*, 23, translation modified.

II. Between breeding and education

1. Campanella's City of the Sun

Behind the first anthropotechnology, namely breeding, stands the Italian Dominican philosopher Tommaso Campanella. Campanella was a revolutionary and a politically engaged activist from around the turn of the 17th century, who organized a wide-reaching movement, supported by the aristocracy as well as by the clergy, that had as its goal the reform of the province of Calabria into a republic, and its liberation from the tyranny of the Spanish crown.[79] The uprising, however, failed and Campanella, who was one of the conspiracy's spiritual heads, was sentenced to serve 27 years in a prison in Naples. During Campanella's imprisonment, he wrote his most famous work, *The City of the Sun* (*Civitas solis*, 1623), which, perhaps unsurprisingly given the circumstances, described a social and political utopia. Like Plato's *Republic* [*Politeiai*], Campanella's utopia is not only a critique of existing social relations and an escape into a distant "City of the Sun"; it is also and above all a text on anthropotechnics. It claims that biological breeding has an enormous but untapped potential with regard to social reform.[80] Campanella's intention is to attempt a planned zoological breeding of human beings. Such breeding strategies were already

---

[79] Germana Ernst, "Tommaso Campanella. Die wissenschaftliche Revolution aus dem Kerker", in *Philosophen der Renaissance. Eine Einführung*, ed. Paul Richard Blum, Darmstadt 1999, 222–236, p. 231; Germana Ernst, *Tommaso Campanella: The Book and the Body of Nature*, Dordrecht 2010.

[80] Cf. Kurt Bayertz, *GenEthics: Technological Intervention in Human Reproduction as a Philosophical Problem*, New York 1995, 19–25; Mika Ojakangas, *On the Greek Origins of Biopolitics: A Reinterpretation of the History of biopower*, London/New York 2016, 135; Rhiannon Noel Welch, *Vital Subjects: Race and Biopolitics in Italy*, Liverpool 2016, 113–114; Armando Maggi, "Tommaso Campanella's Philosophy and the Birth of Modern Science", *Modern Philology*, 3 (2010), 475–492.

long-standing practices in the "breed[ing] of horses and dogs".[81] What the author depicts in his *City of the Sun* is a birth politics carried out with the tools of his time and led by the state. Accordingly, it is an anthropotechnical discipline that is applied from outside of the subject rather than from within the subject.

I will primarily consider Campanella's procreative program here, which has a distinctly political character, since in the *City of the Sun* reproduction is a political matter. Campanella's "body politic" is characterized by rigorous rational planning and order. The executives of the state, whether they appear in the person of the doctor, the astrologer, or the politician, are always men. All anthropotechnics is conceived in terms of a goal, be this goal the moral man, the "whole" man, or a higher and healthier "race". For Campanella, the goal of anthropotechnics is the good and the healthy, as well as the furnishing of offspring for the state. Its fundamental principle is that procreation exists for "the preservation of the species and not for individual pleasure" and that "the breeding of children has reference to the commonwealth, and not to individuals, except in so far as they are constituents of the commonwealth."[82] The citizen lacks a precise "plan," because he reproduces "without purpose," and thereby only contributes to the "destruction" of the state.[83] Securing productive reproduction is therefore "with reference to the good of the commonwealth and not individuals."[84] The responsibility for creating offspring lies in the hands of the state. Therefore, men and women must be matched to one another "according to philosophical rules" and in such a way as to bring forth "the best offspring."[85] The application of large-scale planning and order to reproduction and education ought, according to Campanella, to prevent the impoverishment of the commonwealth, which occurs when the laws of re-

---

[81] Tommaso Campanella, "Sonnenstaat", in Klaus J. Heinisch (Ed.), *Der utopische Staat: Morus, Utopia/Campanella, Sonnenstaat/Bacon, Neu-Atlantis*, Hamburg 1993, 100–150, p. 122ff; "City of the Sun", in Henry Morley (Ed.), *Ideal Commonwealths; Plutarch's Lycurgus, More's Utopia, Bacon's New Atlantis, Campanella's City of the Sun*, London 1890, 236. For information on the manuscript and edition see Nina Chordas, *Forms in Early Modern Utopia: The Ethnography of Perfection*, Fernham 2010, 113. In cases where the English translation did not contain all the original sentences, the German edition was used.

[82] Campanella, "Sonnenstaat," 133; "City of the Sun", 238.

[83] Ibid., 235.

[84] Ibid., 236.

[85] Ibid., 236, 224.

production are neglected, or when men engage in sexual intercourse without consideration of time, place, or choice of sexual partner. One must apply one's principal and entire care to reproduction, and natural characteristics must be contemplated, rather than "riches and rank."[86] This theory seems relatively modern insofar as "natural characteristics" stand in contrast to the rule of a blood aristocracy. The aristocrat, according to his biological endowment, is no better than the simple bourgeois. Accordingly, in Campanella, virtues come from "predisposition" and not from "effort" of any kind.[87] Since everything finds its way back to biological endowment, it follows that men are biologically determined. On the one hand, this would seem to be tyranny *par excellence*; on the other hand, the "planner" of human optimization is granted autonomy.[88] This breeder conceives of human beings as malleable "building blocks" of biological material whom he puts together according to his own calculations. Man becomes an experiment and an object. We will notice the emergence of a similar notion around 1900 in the work of the educational reformer Ellen Key. The collective is primary, the individual, by contrast, becomes an object, hidden in the anonymous 'one'. The ethicist Hans Jonas states a justified critique of this model when he writes that "what is wrong with making a person an experimental subject is not so much that we make him thereby a means (which happens in social contexts of all kinds), as that we make him a thing – a passive thing merely to be acted on [...]."[89] But this reification and objectification of human being is symptomatic of any anthropotechnics, hence the biopolitical expression *"Fiat experimentum in corpore vili."* What the German doctor Julius Pagel stated in 1905, with his maxim of "carry[ing] out experiments only on worthless bodies" is far more true of the medical and eugenicist experiments of his time than it is of Campanella's utopian vision.[90] However, even the early modern thinkers first had to devalue the body, objectify it, and deprive it of its freedom in order to then utilize it in the city of the sun. At the same time, bodies must be *de-coded* so that they can be politically *re-coded*. In Campanella too, there are *corpora vila*, such

---

[86] Ibid., 132, 225.

[87] Ibid.

[88] Ibid.

[89] Hans Jonas, "Philosophical Reflections on Experimenting with Human Subjects", *Daedalus* 98 (1969), 219–246, p. 235.

[90] Julius Pagel, "Über den Versuch am lebenden Menschen", *Deutsche Aerzte-Zeitung*, 10/1905, 217–228, p. 226. The saying "Fiat experimentum in corpore vili" supposedly goes back to the French humanist Marc Antoine Muret (1526–1585).

as the barren women who are explicitly made into public property. Anyone is permitted to "experiment" on them. In Campanella, human experiments are coded according to the ethical distinction of "worthless" and "worthy", which is nothing other than "object" and "subject."

When human beings are understood to be things, they can be used and disposed of without difficulty. A biologically determining intervention is only possible in relation to future generations. In this sense, the processes and rites of reproduction are so important to Campanella that he establishes a whole system of rules around them. These rules prescribe strict imperatives as to who is allowed to pair off with whom and when. So "no woman [...] can be joined to any man before she reaches the age of nineteen."[91] The man must be at least 21 years old. Any man who has not had sexual intercourse before he is 21, or even 27, is to be celebrated in public gatherings with "honors and songs."[92] The medicalization of bodily discourse contains the promise of a greater maturity and hygiene. If a man wishes to engage in sexual intercourse before his 21st birthday – something women are forbidden to do – he is only permitted to do so with "outcast" women, be they "barren or pregnant", in order to avoid a compulsion to "unnatural outlets".[93] This permission is granted by a supervising doctor. A clear utilitarianism can be seen here. Politics, religion, and science are intertwined and intermeshed. On this model, officials are also priests and "scientific teachers".[94] In contrast to Giorgio Agamben, who sees the border between a thanatopolitics and a biopolitics as becoming increasingly blurred, we can already see the convergency of these two tendencies in Campanella's blueprint. In Agamben, the border between thanatopolitics and biopolitics is "in motion and gradually moving into areas other than that of political life, areas in which the sovereign is entering into an ever more intimate symbiosis not only with the jurist but also with the doctor, the scientist, the expert, and the priest."[95] In the city of the sun, where so much depends on fertility and birth, the crimes that are most severely punished are those that are committed against procreation. Hence the punishment for sodomy ranges from public humiliation all the way up to the death penalty for re-

---

[91] Campanella, "Sonnenstaat", 131.
[92] Ibid.
[93] Ibid.
[94] Ibid., 132.
[95] Compare Giorgio Agamben, *Homo Sacer. Sovereign Power and Bare Life*, Stanford 1998, 122.

peat offenders. He who offends against procreation and "overturns order" is an enemy of the state.[96]

In the thirteenth chapter of Campanella's tract, he asks how men and women "can best pass along their bodily inheritance."[97] He takes the Spartans as his example, who trained in the sports arena naked. According to Campanella, men and women should also be naked when they are assembled under the supervision of officials. The natural body – unclothed – can then be observed as an aesthetic artifact. The material body thus becomes considered in the light of a normative criterion that connects like with like. The reasoning behind this is that two capable and good human beings, or bodies, will produce even more capable and good progeny. "Large and beautiful women will be joined only with large and capable men, fat women with skinny men, and scrawny women with strong-bodied men, so that they successfully balance one another out."[98] For Campanella, nothing is more important than physical beauty: "Through regular exercise a woman's body gets a lively color and forceful, strong, well-toned limbs. A well-formed and well-toned build is the ideal of beauty."[99] In Campanella's *City of the Sun*, then, one's biological inheritance is immediately visible. "Behind this notion lies the conviction that a human being's 'natural characteristics' are fundamentally part of his social qualities, and that they can only be acquired genetically."[100] On the one hand, the author wants to produce a highly bred class of the good and the capable. On the other hand, what follows is a study in a prescriptive mediocrity where the antipodes (thick and thin) find one another, so that the resulting children will approach the desired norm. Anyone who misrepresents themselves to their spouse also betrays the state. "For this reason, any woman who applies cosmetics to her face in order to appear beautiful, or wears high heels in order to appear taller, or dresses with trains to cover her deformed feet will be sentenced to death."[101]

When couples are brought together to perform sexual intercourse, the act is planned and structured down to its last details. Medical-religious

---

[96] Campanella, "Sonnenstaat", 131.

[97] Ibid.

[98] Ibid.

[99] Ibid., p. 134.

[100] Bayertz, *GenEthics: Technological Intervention in Human Reproduction as a Philosophical Problem*, 26.

[101] Campanella, "Sonnenstaat", 133ff.

laws come into effect well in advance of the coupling itself. The sexual praxis is arranged so that in the three days prior to intercourse both the man and the woman refrain from any sexual act. Their bodies must be as pure as their souls: this is necessary for their "reconciliation with God."[102] The hour of the union is determined medically as well as by the natural sciences, that is, by an astrologer and a doctor who "attempt to find the time in which Venus and Mercury have entered into a favorable house, to the east of the sun."[103] All later "predisposition" is determined by these medical-astrological criteria. "It is from [these criteria] that the origin of the life forces and of the harmony of the whole with the individual parts of the collective destiny arises."[104] Science, which in Campanella's *City of the Sun* has a religious basis, attempts to design a perfect apparatus for birth and reproduction. The city-state strives for an absolute planning that in its turn assumes full disciplinary control over the body. "Sculptures of famous men" are placed in the bedroom for women's mental and aesthetic edification.[105] This doctrine of imagination rests on the contemporaneous assumption that emotionally charged sense-impressions can have an immediate influence "on the development and form of the child."[106] Campanella's logic operates on the level of analogies arranged according to the episteme of "similarity" which was analyzed by Foucault in *The Order of Things* as the central schema of the Renaissance.[107] The underlying belief in Campanella's text is that the mother's impressions can be inscribed into the child. The above-mentioned reproductive laws are valid only for "normal", fertile men willing to procreate. These prescriptions do not hold for men who, whether for pleasure or for reasons of health, engage in sexual intercourse "with a barren or pregnant woman" or a prostitute.[108] Nonetheless, insofar as worthless bodies, as objects, belong to the state too, they are also contained by this sexual *dispositif*. According to Foucault, the "sexual *dispositif*" that emerges here justifies its existence in the bodies that it multiplies, renews, brings together, invents, and penetrates in greater and greater detail, and in the fact that its control of the population becomes

---

[102] Ibid., 131.

[103] Ibid., 132.

[104] Ibid.

[105] Ibid., 131.

[106] Lisa Malich, "Zeitpfeile, Zeitfaltung und Diskursanalyse: zu Kontinuitäten der Imaginationslehre", *Berichte zur Wissenschaftsgeschichte*, 4 (2011), 363–378, p. 365.

[107] Foucault, *The Order of Things*, 19–50.

[108] Campanella, "Sonnenstaat", 131.

more and more global. This *dispositif* is the basis of a bio-power that is applied "at the level of life, the species, the race, and the large-scale phenomena of population."[109] In this sense, the "lawless" body can be grasped as a controllable thing that is also capable of providing service to the state.

To see Campanella as the forerunner of a eugenicist biology, which can be read in the literary discourse of his time, that is, a biology that is medically grounded, does not seem to be entirely wide of the mark. It is all too clear that for Campanella what is paramount is the anthropotechnic perfection of reproduction. This classical biology is consequently a purely programmatic experimental praxis based entirely on sexual reproduction. To that end, the best possible progeny are achieved by means of positive selection. Thus Campanella is a figure, appearing already in the early modern period, who, in his anthropotechnical tableau, postulates a belief in the power of biological disposition that is just as strong as when this notion emerges in the discourse of the 20th century for the first time. Unlike education, breeding is not applied to the child, but to its parents. Whereas education aims at developing consciousness, breeding is concerned with the biological difference that is inherited from the parents' biological predisposition. By thinking offspring and political power together, as Campanella does, anything that threatens the progeny becomes, by the same token, an attack on the state. In cases where the joining of a man and a woman would "endanger" the progeny, their sexual union is decreed impermissible by a doctor in the city of the sun.[110]

In conclusion, we can say that Campanella's anthropotechnics is marked by its goal being the medical and scientific control of birth, command of which lies with the state. Consequently, all the individual details of marital sexuality are strictly ritualized in his utopia: children are bred for the preservation of the species and not individual pleasure. The collective must be well-bred. Armando Maggi says that "the philosopher's utopia of the *City of the Sun* is based on Campanella's view of 'natural law'. Its inhabitants, called 'Solars' (*Solari*), though ignorant of Christ's message, share everything, including their women, with whom men mate only according to the strict rules of eugenics, and not to express private love."[111]

---

[109] Michel Foucault, *The History of Sexuality Vol. 1: The Will to Knowledge*, trans. Robert Hurley, London 1998, 137.

[110] Campanella, "Sonnenstaat", 135.

[111] Maggi, "Tommaso Campanella's Philosophy and the Birth of Modern Science", 485.

The use of the utopian literary form by Campanella is entirely fitting, because this "no place" (οὐ τόπος; *ou topos*) demands sacrifice. Consequently, there is no room for love in Campanella's vision. "Utopia always comes at the cost of actual life."[112] The sick and the weak are rigorously weeded out and "the permission to marry functions as a breeding-measure."[113] This perfectionist intervention into biological materials cannot be realized through education or schooling, but rather through the fine-tuning of the selection of spouses. As a result, breeding and the penal system are of much greater significance for Campanella than the educational system. In his view, the right bodies must be brought together at the right time, at the right place and in the right manner in order to produce the best possible progeny.

2. Kant's Theory of Education

Around about 1800 – that is, 200 years after Campanella – philosophical thinking in Central Europe distanced itself from the notion of biological breeding. Nonetheless, anthropotechnics was by no means abandoned. It only became more subtle. Immanuel Kant represents the first chapter in the history of an education oriented by Enlightenment values and norms.

In Kant, unlike in Campanella, anthropotechnics is not achieved through biological breeding or heredity. Anthropotechnics rather concerns a cognitive change that takes place "from the inside" out, that is, a transformation of disposition and thought.

Between 1776 and 1784, Kant gave lectures four times on pedagogy at the University of Königsberg. Inspired by Rousseau's *Émile*, Kant was preoccupied with anthropological thought. The very first sentence of *On Pedagogy* already shows how Kant sees the idea of education: "The human being is the only creature who must be educated."[114] By education, Kant understands "care" (maintenance, support), "discipline" (training),

---

[112] Heiner Müller, *Jenseits der Nation*, Berlin 1991, 70. Müller continues: "It makes no difference what philosophy a society that is serious about utopia refers to – it inevitably mobilizes religious energies. Without the Messiah there is no utopia, [...]" (ibid., 75).

[113] Gehring, "Zwischen Menschenpark und Soft eugenics", S. 157.

[114] Immanuel Kant, "Über Pädagogik", in Kant, *Gesammelte Werke, Akademieausgabe* (AA), ed. Preussischen Akademie der Wissenschaften, Vol. 9, Berlin 1900ff, 441; Immanuel Kant, *Anthropology from a Pragmatic Point of View*, trans. and ed. Robert B. Louden, New York 2010; Robert B. Louden, *Kant's Impure Ethics: From Rational Be-*

and "instruction, together with formation [Bildung]."[115] It is said, following Kant, that man is "first infant, then pupil, then apprentice."[116] Unlike animals, however, human beings lack instincts. *Homo sapiens* is thus seen by Kant not as an *animal rationale* but rather as an *animal rationabile*, a living being that *can* be reasonable. This kernel of Kant's *Anthropology from a Pragmatic Point of View* turns on the question of what man *can* make of himself. For Kant "pragmatic" means that which is directly useful for "skillfulness."[117] "Pragmatic anthropology" is therefore an applied theory of the human being, since it claims to prescribe "rules of behavior."[118] Kant defines the object of "anthropology" as "to become civilized through culture."[119] Consequently, it is a matter of differentiating between nature and culture, factuality from conception. Kant goes on to list four types of education: discipline, cultivation, civilization, and finally, morality, the last as a kind of meta-education. First and foremost, man needs to be trained (Zucht) and given direction.[120] With this foundation, he can then be educated and reared, because it is discipline (Zucht) that "changes animal nature into human nature."[121] Such domestication technologies require educators, who must themselves be rigorously educated. Here a paradox can be seen in Kant's pedagogy, because what education wants above all else is to train reasonable and free individuals. Nonetheless, it must utilize compulsion to drive out savagery. An enlightened education can and, at the same time, must not command. Maturity cannot be commanded, because such a command is self-refuting. Kant recognizes this paradoxical fragmentation of the pedagogical discourse: "One of the biggest problems of education is how one can unite submission under lawful constraint with the capacity to use one's freedom. For constraint is necessary. How do I

---

ings to Human Beings, New York 2000. In cases where the English translation did not contain all the original sentences, the German edition was used.

[115] Ibid.

[116] Ibid.

[117] Kant, AA 9: 450; Louden, *Kant's Impure Ethics: From Rational Beings to Human Beings*, 40.

[118] Kant, AA 7: 176, 189, 323; *Anthropology from a Pragmatic Point of View*, 228.

[119] Ibid.

[120] For this translation of the German term 'Zucht' cf. Louden, *Kant's Impure Ethics: From Rational Beings to Human Beings*, 39.

[121] Kant, AA 9: 441.

cultivate freedom under constraint?"[122] Kant's solution lies in the fact that even these early barriers ("the inevitable resistance of society"[123]) lead the child to his own freedom while, on the other hand, it must be demonstrated to the student that he must let the process of pedagogical discipline run its course in order to attain his freedom. "Therefore the human being must be accustomed early to subject himself to the precepts of reason."[124] Subjection is meant here metaphorically, as Kant's reference to the animal, which represents savagery (as distinct from rawness), suggests. Through use of his freedom man can become savage; the animal, because of its instincts, cannot. Kant says that the man who "is uncultured is raw; he who is undisciplined is savage."[125] This wildness consists of "independence from laws."[126] Laws are for Kant a cultural foundation that he, unlike Rousseau, regards as constant. The anthropotechnics of taming (which takes the form of a bodily discipline) is seen as coextensive with, as well as preceding, Kant's concept of education. Students need discipline "that they may grow accustomed to sitting still and observing punctually what they are told."[127] Here education and the institution of the school are plainly instruments of domestication. Kant's philanthropic manner of considering this question obscures this domesticizing aspect of education. Sloterdijk correctly observes that in this sense pedagogy recounts the shared history of children and animals. "Behind the educator, one recognizes the barely disguised figure of the animal tamer – just as there is grooming behind all teaching."[128] Sloterdijk goes further still and shows that anthropotechnics are in no way limited to school. Because, in actual fact, "all the world is a school – and all humans merely pupils."[129] Kant's discipline also teaches submission as well as usefulness, since the trained body becomes the goal of education. The "laboratory of the body" is also in this sense an experimental object of knowledge and power.[130] Power does not censor knowledge, but rather

---

[122] Ibid., 453. Cf. also Chris W. Surprenant, *Kant and the Cultivation of Virtue*, Abingdon 2014, 76–107.

[123] Ibid.

[124] Ibid., 442.

[125] Ibid.

[126] Ibid.

[127] Ibid., 441.

[128] Sloterdijk, *Du mußt dein Leben ändern*, 311; *You must change your life*, 198.

[129] Ibid., 551ff; *You must change your life*, 350.

[130] Kant, *Gesammelte Schriften*, Berlin 1997, Vol. 25: *Vorlesungen über Anthropologie*, 145.

produces it. Hence it is only by means of "power over the body that a physiological, organic knowledge of it became possible."[131] In a certain sense, then, knowledge is always embodied.

During the *ancien régime*, in particular, the "perfection" of the body by means of education was the order of the day. As early as the 16th century, the children of the court was expected to pay strict attention to the way they carried their bodies. Every child had to observe each of his movements and correct his posture accordingly. Physical "uprightness" belonged to the culture of courtesy.[132] A microphysics of power began to inscribe itself onto the body, thereby turning the body into art. "The body presents itself like a painting, at that point where all lines of sight converge."[133] The French historian Robert Muchembled points out an expression that dominated an entire society like no other, right down to the roots of its speech: "One must cut a good figure."[134] Foucault would dedicate an entire book to this discipline of the "good figure". In *Discipline and Punish*, he places disciplinary power at the center of his analysis, right beside the panoptical system of punishment, the latter being a disciplinary power that circulates not only in "unfree" punishments, like the prison, but also in the military, as well as in humanist educational programs. "The historical moment of the disciplines was the moment when an art of the human body was born, which was directed not only at the growth of its skills, nor at the intensification of its subjection, but at the formation of a relation that in the mechanism itself makes it more obedient as it becomes more useful, and conversely."[135]

What Kant describes with his description of "sitting still" is therefore a direct anthropotechnics carried out on the body itself. The body becomes an object in the "laboratory."[136] In this way, not only is a rhythm trained into the body, but each individual activity is separated into the smallest units of time, while body and gesture become interconnected. This ongo-

---

[131] Michel Foucault, "Body/Power", in *Power/Knowledge: Selected Interviews and Other Writings by Michel Foucault*, ed. Colin Gordon, New York 1980, 55–62, p. 59.
[132] Michael Muchembled, *Die Erfindung des modernen Menschen. Gefühlsdifferenzierung und kollektive Verhaltensweisen des Absolutismus*, Hamburg 1990, 228. Cf. Sara E. Melzer and Kathryn Norberg (Ed.), *From the Royal to the Republican Body: Incorporating the Political in Seventeenth and Eighteenth-Century France*, Berkeley 1998.
[133] Ibid.
[134] Ibid.
[135] Michel Foucault, *Discipline and Punish*, trans. Alan Sheridan, New York 1995, 137.
[136] Kant, *Vorlesungen über Anthropologie*, 145.

ing drilling of learned ability has an increasing submission as its result. We thus arrive at the aforementioned paradox, namely that seemingly "harmless" reading is, it could be said, itself a taming technique. The reader cannot struggle – that is the simple and illuminating substance of the argument. Reading can be seen as within the tradition of meditation. Man is to arrive at an interiorization of bodily discipline. This discipline is something more than sitting still while one reads. It is an entire habitus in which man, little by little, is to "achieve victory over material nature [his own, as well as external nature – K.L.]."[137] Even though Kant did not conceive of the human being as a machine at all, in his conception of discipline precisely this dynamic of the functionalization and instrumentalization of forces on the one hand, as well as an internalized social compulsion to self-restraint on the other, remains. By the end of the process, the student will be able to control his body of his own accord and remain sitting still. There is no longer any need for a teacher after the successful application of this anthropotechnics. The sociologist Pierre Bourdieu states this clearly: "What is 'learned by body' is not something that one has, like knowledge that can be brandished, but something that one is."[138] Norbert Elias notes of the same phenomena that "the control and surveillance apparatus of society" becomes "a control apparatus in the psychic household of the individual."[139] According to Kant, the measure of a normative "training" (Zucht) internalized by the student is nonetheless necessary, because "when he [the student – K.L.] is allowed to have his own way and is in no way opposed in his youth, then he will retain a certain savagery throughout his life."[140] It is only through this politics of the body that man becomes the reasonable citizen he ought to be. The body is a habitus because "its carriage bears traces of its social belonging."[141] Man needs maintenance and education so that he can make something of himself. According to Kant, "formation [Bildung] includes training and instruction."[142] "Maintenance" is used by Kant in a similar way to Sloterdijk, since man is still helpless in

---

[137] Erich Schön, *Der Verlust der Sinnlichkeit oder die Verwandlung des Lesers*, Stuttgart 1987, 94.

[138] Pierre Bourdieu, *The Logic of Practice*, trans. Richard Nice, New York 1990, 73. Cf. Quang Gao, "Bourdieu and Body", in Lisa Hunter, Wayne Smith and Elke Emerald (Ed.), *Pierre Bourdieu and Physical Culture*, London/New York 2015, 143–148.

[139] Norbert Elias, *Über den Prozess der Zivilisation*, Frankfurt a. M. 1997, Vol. 2, 338.

[140] Kant, AA 9: 438.

[141] Muchembled, *Die Erfindung des modernen Menschen*, 229.

[142] Kant, AA 9: 443.

comparison to animals. He is "animalistically immature" and thus fails in his "being an animal".[143] The view of many 20th-century philosophical anthropologists (among them Helmuth Plessner and Arnold Gehlen), namely that men, unlike animals, must become something, can already be found in Kant. At birth, man is nothing. Plessner, for all intents and purposes, continues Kant's line of thinking when he says that man "truly has nothing to stand on," since "he lives only insofar as he leads a life."[144] What he means is that man is nothing particularly special with respect to his biological abilities, sensory organs and his motor skills. And hence Gehlen, echoing Herder, calls man a "creature of defects" (Mängelwesen).[145] According to Nietzsche, humans are "the still undetermined animals."[146] Nietzsche's emphasis here falls on the "still" that remains to be worked out. A *techne* (an "art of man") must be applied to human beings.

In Kant, this technology takes the form of a four-part rational education. He formulates all of the aforementioned problems and maxims of anthropotechnics in a particularly succinct expression: "The human being can only become a human being through education. He is nothing except what education makes out of him. It must be noted that the human being is only educated by other human beings, human beings who likewise have been educated."[147] But Kant also sees a stumbling block in the error-prone human being as educator, for "if some day a being of a higher kind were to look after our education, then one would see what the human being could become."[148]

- First: from birth on, man is not a moral being, or a being that is any way defined.

---

[143] Sloterdijk, *Menschenpark*, 34.

[144] Helmuth Plessner, *Die Stufen des Organischen und der Mensch. Einleitung in die philosophische Anthropologie* (1928), Berlin/New York 1975, 293, 384; *Levels of Organic Life and the Human: An Introduction to Philosophical Anthropology*, trans. Millay Hyatt, New York 2019. For a good overview Gerald Hartung, *Philosophische Anthropologie, Grundwissen Philosophie*, 2. Ed., Stuttgart 2018.

[145] Arnold Gehlen, *Der Mensch*, Wiesbaden 1986, 20; Johann Gottfried Herder, *Abhandlung über den Ursprung der Sprache*, Stuttgart 1993, 24.

[146] Nietzsche, KSA 5, 38; *Beyond Good and Evil: Prelude to a Philosophy of the Future*, trans. Judith Norman, New York 2002, 62.

[147] Kant, AA 9: 443.

[148] Ibid.

- Second: he needs an anthropotechnics in order to be able to live at all socially in a rational society.

- Third: man cannot be educated by a higher entity, but must educate himself.

In Kant's view, pedagogy contains a singular possibility: changing man down to his very roots, "for behind education lies the secret of the perfection [Vollkommenheit] of human nature."[149] The teleological hope of Enlightenment reform is that man can become better through education. This education is the "prospect of a future happier human species."[150] Through education, man can make himself more than he is and let the "germ" of his "vocation" sprout.[151] However, Kant calls these ideas of transformation an "ideal," because he realizes the process of man's completion could only slowly be realized.[152]

As these citations show, what is typical of classical anthropotechnics is the forming of an entire collective (a race, a society). This is in contrast to modern genetic anthropotechnics, which concerns the individual. For Kant it is "not individual human beings, but rather the human species shall get there" (i.e., reach perfection).[153] Anthropotechnics is subordinate to the dimension of time, specifically of the future, here. Accordingly, "education [is] an art, the practice of which must be perfected over generations."[154] Kant is aware of just how much depends on this basic formulation, since, with it, the whole enterprise can either succeed or fail. It is a crossroads for the human race: "If one thinks this over carefully, one finds that it is very difficult. That is why education is the greatest and most difficult problem that can be given to the human being. For education depends on insight and insight depends on education."[155] This paradoxical chiasmus is at the core of Kant's educational program.

When the various anthropotechnics in Kant that are subsumed under the methodological heading of "education" are examined more closely, it can

---

[149] Ibid., 444.
[150] Ibid.
[151] Ibid., 445.
[152] So he realizes that our "species seems to fare no better in achieving its vocation with respect to *happiness* [...]." (Kant, AA 7: 326; *Anthropology from a Pragmatic Point of View*, 231).
[153] Kant, AA 9: 445.
[154] Ibid., 446.
[155] Ibid.

be noted that the art of education does not simply proceed "mechanically", without a plan, but rather "judiciously", as Kant puts it, according to certain principles.[156] Kant wants to make pedagogy into a science through this judicious procedure, a science that, transcending theory, will also allow for educational experiments ("the laboratory of the body"). Science, as Heidegger's student, the philosopher Hans-Georg Gadamer says, is based "on a knowledge [that is] directed toward doing, and being able to do, a knowing mastery of nature that is a technology."[157] In Kant's technical education, knowledge and practice become a practical knowing and a knowing practice.

The four anthropotechnics that Kant lays out categorically, and that constitute the paradox between constraint and freedom in Kant's pedagogy, can now be examined more closely. The first category is *discipline*. For Kant, "discipline" means the attempt to "prevent animality from doing damage to humanity; both in the individual and in society."[158] Thus discipline is "merely the taming of savagery."[159] The second category is *cultivation*. Cultivation "is the procurement of skillfulness."[160] Kant brings together cultural techniques like reading and writing under this heading. He proposes "civilizing" as a third technique. By this he means a kind of "civilizing" whose "prerequisites are good behavior and a certain prudence."[161] The concept "civilizing" means forming oneself to the conditions of the present. The fourth and last category is the most significant, since in it the Enlightenment goal of Kant's project comes into view: *moralization*. "The human being should not merely be skilled for all sorts of ends, but should also acquire the disposition to choose nothing but good ends."[162] Thus man will learn to be able to choose his actions morally. Although this task appears to be a phase of education, it is nonetheless moralization that ultimately confers meaning on the other three. This moralization is the central point of Kant's concept of education. Every pedagogy must be based on this principle. Man must not simply be educated according to these first

---

[156] Ibid., 447.
[157] Hans-Georg Gadamer, "Theorie, Technik, Praxis – die Aufgabe einer neuen Anthropologie", in Hans Georg Gadamer and Paul Vogler (Ed.), *Neue Anthropologie*, Vol. 1. *Biologische Anthropologie*, IX–XXXVII, p. XIII.
[158] Kant, AA 9: 449.
[159] Ibid.
[160] Ibid.
[161] Ibid., 450.
[162] Ibid.

three goals and become a well-behaved machine. He must also become truly rational and moral. In this respect, moralization, which stands at the end of Kant's pedagogy, justifies the element of compulsion in his notion of education. Without morality, there could be no ethical compulsion in training and discipline as Kant understands them. "The human being can be merely trained [dressiert], conditioned, mechanically taught, or actually enlightened."[163] It is in the claim 'The child must learn to think for himself' that Kant sees the difference between a mere domestication and a true education. It quickly becomes clear that here Kant is launching a forceful critique of his own time, which has merely been trained (dressiert), and therefore been subjected to a compulsion that has not been justified: "We live in a time of disciplinary training, culture, and civilization, but not by any means in a time of moralization."[164]

By way of summary, one can say that for Kant what is significant is the rational planning of an authoritative education, whose various categories can be applied to man, who must learn discipline and rational thinking. At the end of this process stands a young adult who is able to reflect on his actions as well as on the educational program he has undergone, so that he can become an educator himself. "Everything in education depends on establishing the right principles throughout and making them comprehensible and acceptable to children."[165] The *formal* goal is thus a step-by-step development of all man's natural capacities. The *material* goal, however, is the perfection of man, that is to say, man is to perfect the notion of humanity in his own person. It is only through this educational process that man can step out of his wild, natural state and become a moral being "when his reason raises itself to the concepts of duty and law."[166] The student must be pulled along this path to his maturity and self-determination. "Enlightenment is the human being's emergence from his self-incurred minority. Minority is inability to make use of one's own understanding [...] *Sapere aude!* Have the courage to make use of your *own* understanding."[167] This Enlightenment education is a matter of imparting values and forming society. An anthropotechnics is applied to the individual, but is nonetheless

---

[163] Ibid.
[164] Ibid., 451.
[165] Ibid., 492–493.
[166] Ibid., 492.
[167] Kant, AA 8: 481–482, 35; "An Answer to the Question: What is Enlightenment?", in Kant, *Practical Philosophy*, trans. and ed. Mary J. Gregor, New York 2006, 17.

ultimately directed at a collective. Kantian education thereby avoids the simple drilling of norms and values that merely guarantees a peaceful co-existence. Above all, adolescents must learn to reflect rationally on their own actions and the actions of others. They must themselves be able "to think and to determine their action according to the criterion of its possible universality in the present situation."[168] In Kant, we find an anthropotechnics following the outlook of the world-citizen, a literal education [Erziehung], since education "pulls" [ziehen] a student towards self-sufficient thinking and reflection. "Whether the human is by nature good or evil? He is neither of the two because by nature he is not a moral being at all; he only becomes one when his reason raises itself to the concepts of law and duty."[169]

3. Humboldt's Theory of Bildung

At the same time as Kant was delivering his lectures, Wilhelm von Humboldt was also preoccupied with human education. At first glance, it seems counterintuitive to describe the neo-humanist pedagogue Humboldt's project as an anthropotechnics. That would apparently be to claim that the philanthropist and educational theorist, who influenced the German bourgeoisie and the German educational system as few others have, is in fact the starting point for a "scandalous" conception of education.

Humboldt and the functionalized planning of human beings? That seems inconceivable – and for this reason, a rupture in the argumentation up to now. Nonetheless, when the matter is considered more closely and we push through Humboldt's idealizing and often mystical language, we recognize that, like Campanella (birth politics) and to some extent Kant (rendering pedagogy scientific by means of experimentation), it becomes clear that this education is in no sense purely spiritual. It is also organized according to nature, which lies beneath the spiritual. Mentioning the chemical concept of "elective affinities" [Wahlverwandtschaften] is not unjustified here. According to Grimm's *Dictionary*, in chemistry "elective affinities" denotes a "property of two bodies" whereby "one or both"

---

[168] Dieter-Jürgen Löwisch, "Immanuel Kant II", in Wolfgang Fischer and Dieter-Jürgen Löwisch (Ed.), *Pädagogisches Denken von den Anfängen bis zur Gegenwart*, Darmstadt 1983, 140–153, p. 151.
[169] Kant, AA 9: 492; cf. Surprenant, *Kant and the Cultivation of Virtue*, 105.

have a tendency "to unite" as we will later see.[170] Humboldt's educational philosophy does not seem to be an anthropotechnics because many concepts, such as compulsion, discipline, control, and so on, are omitted, and it is therefore not seen as constituted by an optimizing, intervening *techne*. Through this conceptual cleansing his theory seems to demand nothing except "freedom and a variety of situations for the independent formation of one's own strengths."[171] There does not seem to be a "compulsion to education" in Humboldt's work.[172] Humboldt's fundamental idea is that "education [Bildung] is the stimulation of all of a man's forces, so that these unfold and adapt to the world harmoniously and proportionally as a force of reciprocal interconnection and restriction, leading to a self-determined individuality or personality that, in its ideality and its singularity, makes humanity richer," as Hartmut von Hentig summarizes the argument.[173] Nonetheless, it would be too simple to reduce the ideas of the Prussian Minister to a simple self-sufficiency (the self-formation of personality) or to reduce education to a self-determined goal or means of self-becoming (or, for that matter, of becoming human). We must see that Humboldt's conception, and the fragment from his *Nachlass*, the "Theory of the Education [Bildung] of Man" (1793), have become an influential concept that still impacts our contemporary situation. The ideas of the man who led the Department of Culture and Education at the Prussian Ministry of the Interior have entered into schooling, politics, and the wider world. What must now be investigated is whether it is overhasty to classify Humboldt as an anthropotechnician.

What must be recalled here is what constitutes an anthropotechnics. First, it has a *telos*, a purpose. It strives for a "better" human being or at least a better adjusted, more capable, more moral human race. Second, it proceeds from a *crisis situation* in its present that it hopes to change. Third, it makes use of various *methods* to change human beings according to a rationally devised plan. Humboldt's work must be examined to see if his educational philosophy meets these criteria.

---

[170] Grimm Wörterbuch, Wahlverwandtschaft, Vol. 27, 597–599. Cf. Jeremy Adler, "Goethe's Use of Chemical Theory in his Elective Affinities", in Andrew Cunningham and Nicholas Jardine (Ed.), *Romanticism and the Sciences*, New York 1990, 263–279.

[171] Tilman Borsche, *Wilhelm von Humboldt*, München 1990, 57.

[172] Ibid., 58.

[173] Hartmut von Hentig, *Bildung. Ein Essay*, München 1996, 40.

The crisis that Humboldt has in view is alienation. Man has been fragmented. Unlike the ancient Greeks, modern man only receives a "fragmentary education." Humboldt's image of a complete human being with a "general education" ("Allgemeinbildung") is comprehensible only against the background of this lack. In 1800, a totality is no longer possible because, as Martin Heidegger puts it in his lecture *Kant and the Problem of Metaphysics*: "Being itself has been dispersed into a multiplicity."[174] According to Friedrich Schiller's diagnosis of contemporary culture, modernity had, in contrast to antiquity, become akin to an "ingenious piece of machinery" ("kunstreiches Uhrwerk") from which no living whole can emerge.[175] As in Kant, Schiller's and Humboldt's critiques are also based on a mechanistic conception of man. And hence the task that lies before man is merely the "putting together of infinitely many lifeless parts."[176] The "notion of the rearing of human beings" that is supposed to solve this problem is, according to Phillip Dessauer, thus "the product of an interim period [...], of a crisis."[177] Even though Dessauer approaches this question from a biological perspective, the connection between anthropotechnics and Humboldt's conception of education is clear. Both are characterized by a will to plan and a wish to realize something that has been absent in human history. It is in this sense that the concept of breeding depends on an "end of history."[178] One might say that the goal and the solution that Humboldt envisages are influenced by his image of antiquity: a vision of man as a complete being. The human "I" – which is, on the one hand, the reciprocal effect of one's own receptivity and reactivity, and, on the other hand, one's ability to act as well as to influence, that is, the respective faculties of the understanding, the power of imagination, and the sensory intuition – must complete itself and connect to the world. The concept of self-development, or *Bildung*, refers to this free, active, and general

---

[174] Martin Heidegger, *Kant und das Problem der Metaphysik*, ed. Friedrich-Wilhelm von Herrmann, 6th edition, Frankfurt a. M. 1998, 295; *Kant and the Problem of Metaphysics*, trans. Richard Taft, Bloomington 1997, 207. This citation is from the Davos Disputation with Ernst Cassirer.

[175] Friedrich Schiller, *Werke, Nationalausgabe* (NA), ed. Julius Petersen and Friedrich Beissner, Weimar 1943ff, Vol. 20, *Über die ästhetische Erziehung des Menschen in einer Reihe von Briefen*, letter 6, 323; *On the Aesthetic Education of Man*, trans. Reginald Snell, Mineola/New York 2004, 40.

[176] Ibid.

[177] Philipp Dessauer, *Das binomische Geschichtsbild*, Freiburg im Breisgau 1946, S. 35.

[178] Ibid., 42.

method applied to the self and the world and it therefore differs from an educational "pulling along" [*Er-Ziehung*].

Consequently, the goal for Humboldt is to "complete the cultivation of humanity into a whole."[179] The first and imperative condition is freedom. The training of the individual notwithstanding, Humboldt has once again a collective in view. This is typical of an anthropotechnics. For Humboldt, this collective is not only a race, a society, or a people, but an affirmative conception of "humanity" ("Menschheit"). Man must "create dignity and permanence for his being", particularly through an "other."[180] It is on this path that man can find immortality over the course of generations. That means education (Bildung) is capable of being reproduced and handed down. According to Humboldt, it is "only thus that the [...] lasting permanence of an acquired good is possible, without this, without the reassuring thought of the consequence of refinement (Veredelung) and education (Bildung), the existence of man would be transient, like the existence of plants [...]."[181] Education is what makes man man. It is the tie that connects the past, the present, and the future. Humboldt even goes so far as to insist that the "ultimate task of our being" is to train "the concept of humanity into our person", to conceive of ourselves as a moral whole.[182] We bear, he says, a germ of humanity in us that we must cultivate. However, it is impossible to do this on our own. Man needs nature, the "non-human," for his cultivation.[183] This "non-human" entity is "the world", which is characterized by its extreme multiplicity and independent self-sufficiency and which creates the unity and the entirety of all objects in itself. Man nonetheless needs the blunt force of an object on which to *train* himself, and a bare form, the pure thought of a matter.[184] Man needs a material outside of himself that he can "work on", that he can recognize, that he can use to train himself. Ultimately, man needs a "world outside of himself."[185] What man attempts in this training is, according to Humboldt, to "grasp the world as much as possible and to connect with himself as closely as he can."[186] Insofar

---

[179] Wilhelm von Humboldt, "Theorie der Bildung. Bruchstück", in Humboldt, *Werke*, Vol. 1, ed. Andreas Flitner and Klaus Giel, Darmstadt 2002, 234–240, p. 235.

[180] Ibid.

[181] Ibid., 236.

[182] Ibid.

[183] Ibid., 235.

[184] Ibid.

[185] Ibid.

[186] Ibid.

as man expresses "the form of his spirit" in and through outside objects, he finds his spirit in them once again. We have seen in above the analysis that this concept of "training" cannot be regarded as innocent. Even if Humboldt attempts to disguise the fact, his concept of education (Bildung) nonetheless uses planning and anthropotechnics. Hence Sloterdijk says of training that "if man genuinely produces man, it is precisely not through work and its concrete results [. . .], it is through life in forms of practice [. . .]. Anyone who speaks of human self-production without addressing the formation of human beings in the practising life has missed the point from the outset."[187] Thus man is a "creature that cannot not practice".[188]

Even if this seems too bold a claim, it is not entirely incorrect to speak of planning or of method with regard to Humboldtian education. Even if the Prussian pedagogue does not say so explicitly, we can nonetheless recognize that, for him, planning is central with respect to nature. For Humboldt, education is "natural" in the truest sense of the word. But what does nature want? According to Humboldt, "nature's striving is directed towards something unrestrained."[189] That is, nature (even nature in human beings) demands wholeness. But how can this wholeness be produced, in Humboldt's view? Nature demands the "reciprocal effect" of forces that are not of the same character, precisely so that they can complete each other.[190] "Only in connection can they make a whole."[191] For Humboldt, this bond is more than a simple neutral connection of materials. These forces have "a complementary need to produce a whole by mutual effect."[192] With this, the heart of the Humboldtian idea of education is attained: the principle of action and reaction in nature, for "the secret of nature rests only on action and reaction (*Wechselwirkung*)."[193] Inner and outer, nature and spirit are analogous. For Humboldt, it is undeniable that physical nature makes a single whole and that phenomena in both (nature and spirit) belong to one and the same law.[194] In an almost mystical, Romantic key, Humboldt speaks of a "longing" that one force has for the other, that must be "sat-

---

[187] Sloterdijk, *Du musst dein Leben ändern*, 13–14; *You must change your life*, 4.

[188] Ibid., 643; *You must change your life*, 406.

[189] Wilhelm von Humboldt, "Über den Geschlechterunterschied und dessen Einfluss auf die organische Natur", in *Werke*, Vol. 1, 268–295, p. 268.

[190] Ibid., 269.

[191] Ibid.

[192] Ibid.

[193] Ibid.

[194] Ibid., 271.

isfied" so that the two can "entwine themselves in one another" and form a "harmonious whole".[195] A "longing" joins the forces to one another, an "elective affinity" (Wahlverwandtschaft).[196] This analogy between the "I" and the world, between man and nature, must be kept in view. Nature acts similarly to spirit. It is thus a matter, for Humboldt, of "joining our ego to the world." Is this thought perhaps "too far-fetched?" as Humboldt himself asks.[197] Because how can spirit take into itself something material without itself becoming material? Humboldt is familiar with this problem and notes that when man wants to take the world into himself, he must consider and plan very precisely. If he takes in too little, then he shuts himself within his inner life and he can no longer recognize the world. But when he lets too much of the outside world into himself, then he loses himself in the world. It is "now important that he not lose himself in this alienation, but much more that everything that he undertakes outside of himself shine an illuminating light and a beneficent warmth back into his inner life."[198] A harmonious balance has taken place in which the world and the subject maintain a balance within an economy of forces. To accomplish this productive reciprocity, the spirit must bring itself closer to the "mass of objects."[199] For Humboldt, that means that "material" must be pressed into the "form of spirit". Spirit enters into the world and the world becomes spiritual. "What man necessarily needs, therefore, is a simple object to make possible the reciprocity of his self-sufficiency with his sensibility."[200] Only the world can be this object. It claims man in his whole being and as a unified whole. Man is only completely man where he encounters world. The concept of "nature" and the concept of "education" include each other: an inside and an outside. Humboldt recognized that this polarity of "inside" and "outside" is an essential element of human existence. Hence man has a human nature that can educate and train itself, just as his external nature forms itself and grows. Humboldt chooses, not inappropriately, the image of a mirror. But it is a mirror that does not reflect so much as it completes. It is in this sense that Humboldt, more than any other thinker, stands for the belief that every person must understand himself in

---

[195] Ibid., 279.
[196] Ibid.
[197] Humboldt, "Theorie der Bildung des Menschen", 236.
[198] Ibid., 237.
[199] Ibid.
[200] Ibid.

order to be human. Man in his entirety is the work of his own education, of his own art. Man must compose himself into a harmonic "symphony" so that he can complete himself "wholly" and thereby become useful to society. Education is thus spirit's attempt to become comprehensible to itself. Our education, which requires the world in order to come into being, comes first and foremost from our disclosure of the world to ourselves and this disclosure in turn constitutes our being human, Humboldt claims.

As was mentioned above, Humboldt also draws on anthropotechnics. He too considers man as transforming himself according to his own (and nature's) plan, and as thereby optimizing himself. Humboldt too wants to form man "generally" by means of the objects of the world and ancient languages. His theory becomes praxis and is realized in the Prussian school system, which was meant to take precisely this "general human education" as its goal.[201] As a result, the course of study Humboldt planned rests on "one and the same basis" for every person[202]: "For the spirit of common wage worker and the spirit of the most finely educated man must, at the outset, be brought into accord in the same way [...]."[203]

In Erich Weber's formulation of the underlying essence of "education" [Bildung], "education cannot be exclusively or excessively based on the intellect, but must rather grasp, claim, and promote man in his entirety (as a head, as a heart, and as a hand)."[204]

That this conception of education also possesses distinct political features is obvious from the fact that Humboldt was employed by the Prussian state. For Humboldt, the task of the state was to secure the best possible means for unfolding the individual's personality. Humboldt's normative idea of a human self-cultivation fits surprisingly well with Sloterdijk's remark in The Human Zoo: "Man has become the higher power for man."[205] He must make something of himself, must "work" on himself. It is again a

---

[201] Wilhelm von Humboldt, "Der Litauische und der Königsberger Schulplan", in Lothar Schweim (Ed.), Schulreform in Preußen 1809–1819, Weinheim 1966, 12–15, p. 14. Cf. Florian Schui, Rebellious Prussians: Urban Political Culture under Frederick the Great and his Successors, Oxford 2013, 176–194.

[202] Ibid., 29.

[203] Ibid., 30.

[204] Erich Weber, Pädagogik. Eine Einführung. Bd. 1: Grundfragen und Grundbegriffe. Teil 3: Pädagogische Grundvorgänge und Zielvorstellungen – Erziehung und Gesellschaft/Politik, Donauwörth 1999, 440.

[205] Sloterdijk, Menschenpark, 45; The Human Zoo, 45.

matter of a technology of the self, which contains a crucial aesthetic component.

4. Education vs. Bildung

If Kant, the Enlightenment philosopher, is to be compared to Humboldt, the neo-humanist, it must first be recognized that here there are differences of degree and not of kind, because both thinkers' proposals for human optimization refer to the spirit and morality. Consequently, their goals are similar: the idea of humanity must be realized within the individual.

The work of both thinkers can be classified under the heading of education. This distinction separates them methodologically from breeding, which is for the most part applied before birth and is conceived of as a biological intervention. Nonetheless Humboldt and Kant part ways in their respective discourses on education in two respects. Both want to bring about a fundamental change in man's cognitive being and make him "more humanistic" as well as "more moral." Nonetheless, unlike Kant, Humboldt puts significant emphasis on the cultivation of man free of any goal. Humboldt's goal is a fundamental general education instead of disciplinary specialization. In Humboldt's pedagogy, "the child is to be formed into a man, not an apprentice shoemaker into a master. That is the new task of all generational education in state schools and that is why this new education is called humanistic."[206] Free education (Bildung), unattached to any goal, only means, however, that education (Bildung) serves no heteronomous goals. The end goal remains man's freedom, as well as training to become a complete human being. Since *Bildung* is its own goal, Kant's three pedagogical anthropotechnics (discipline, cultivation, civilization) have no place in Humboldt's work. Humboldt's model works without compulsion – it is rather characterized by man's anthropological striving towards education and *Bildung*.[207] Humboldt teases out this point in a letter to Georg

---

[206] Vgl. Humboldt, *Werke in fünf Bänden*, ed. Andreas Flitner and Klaus Giel. Darmstadt 1961–1980, Vol. 4, 60.

[207] Humboldt seems to have had an "art of living" in mind here. He wrote this to Caroline at least at the end of 1796 (cf. Rudolf Freese, "Wilhelm von Humboldts Bildungs- und Humanitätsidee", in Rudolf Hoberg (Ed.), *Sprache und Bildung. Beiträge zum 150. Todestag Wilhelm von Humboldts*, Darmstadt 1987, 13–52, p. 22). The "art of living", as it is later conceptualized by Foucault and Schmid, is discussed in the following chapters, but Humboldt can be read in a similar direction.

Forster of 16 August 1791 when he writes that "the first law of a true morality is: form yourself, and its second is: act onto others and onto yourself thereby."[208]

It is thus through this inner will that Humboldt's analysis is able to shake off the problem of compulsion that is so prevalent in Kant. On the other hand, through its mystical language, as well as its emphasis on dominance based on the purely inward striving of the subject, Humboldt's model takes on its own dynamic and gives rise to a rational system of rules. This system of structure-giving categories can also be encountered in Kant, who furnishes the three aforementioned anthropotechnic methods. Where Humboldt defines "the most general, the most active, and the most free mutual relationship" between the self and the world, between the subject of *Bildung* and the substance of *Bildung* as a dialectic of form and material[209], Kant develops an education [*Erziehung*] in the sense of a "pulling along" that assumes the presence of a moral, enlightened educator who takes the student on. This difference can be expressed by saying that in Humboldt the self and the world are side by side, on the same level, and affect one another reciprocally. In Kant, on the other hand, there is a natural hierarchy between teacher and student. And here the fundamental difference between self-cultivation, as *Bildung*, and education, *Erziehung*, emerges: self-cultivation is, for Humboldt, something natural, something that develops *from* man and *through* him, an inner germ that the self, with the aid of an outside object, can make blossom and grow. Self-cultivation is more strongly tied to the autonomous cognition and activity of the individual who undertakes it. Education [*Erziehung*], on the other hand, as can be discerned from the etymology of the German term, describes a process of 'pulling along' [*ziehen*] towards a fixed goal.[210] The person who does the pulling is already at the goal and must pull the student along towards it, sometimes forcefully. Education in this sense has no strong basis in individual intention or in anthropological striving. Kant defines this type of cultivation as "training and instruction" ("Zucht und Unterweisung").[211]

---

[208] Humboldt to Forster, 16. 8. 1791, in *Wilhelm v. Humboldt im Verkehr mit seinen Freunden*, ed. Theodor Knappstein, Berlin 1917, S. 34.

[209] Humboldt, "Theorie der Bildung des Menschen", 235ff.

[210] 'Educate' goes back to Old German 'irziohan' ('to pull out') and under the model of the word 'educare' (Latin for 'to raise', 'to feed', 'to educate') soon takes on the feudal meaning "to form someone's spirit and character and to promote his development" (cf. Duden: *Dictionary of Origin. Etymology of the German language*, 4. Ed. 2007).

[211] Kant AA 9: 443.

Both Kant and Humboldt are quite close to one another in using the traditional image of the wise gardener who must intervene when the young plant is not growing correctly. However, Kant always conceives of this intervention as taking place from outside: "A tree which stands alone in the field grows crooked and spreads its branches wide. By contrast, a tree which stands in the middle of a forest grows straight towards the sun and air above it, because the trees that stand next to it offer opposition."[212] It follows, in Kant's view, that man can never become entirely complete. Nonetheless, he must approach this completeness. "Out of such crooked wood as the human being, nothing entirely straight can be fabricated."[213]

Kant, like Humboldt, attempts to create a free space for the individual in which he can develop himself. There is nonetheless a directed development for Kant, with the assistance of external instances and rules. For Humboldt, on the other hand, we find a freer unfolding that tends towards an individual, humanistic self-cultivation guided by the self. In Sloterdijk's formulation, humanism begins with the assumption "that humanity itself consists in choosing to develop one's nature through the media of taming, and to forswear bestialization."[214] For Humboldt, man himself selects the correct literature (be it Greek or any other that promotes education) as a prescriptive text and "world," while for Kant, on the other hand, the correct media are prepared by the educator. The difference between the two lies in the activity and passivity of the selection, and not in the goal of optimization itself, which they both share. This anthropological feature of self-domestication becomes quite prominent if we characterize man as "an organism that domesticates itself and that subdues itself with a challenge or a call."[215]

---

[212] Ibid., 448.
[213] Kant AA 8: 23.
[214] Sloterdijk, *Menschenpark*, 19; *The Human Zoo*, 16.
[215] Plessner, *Die Stufen des Organischen und der Menschen*, 317.

5. The "categorical imperatives of the nerves and the blood"

1. Between Pet and Child

> "Thus I love only my children's land, the undiscovered land in the furthest sea: for it I command my sails to seek and seek.
>
> I want to make it up to my children for being the child of my fathers; and to all the future – for the existence of this present.
>
> All parents who hope, in the new century to form the new man."
>
> (Nietzsche, Thus Spoke Zarathustra) [216]

In the text *Barnets århundrade* (*The Century of the Child*), which was written in 1900 by the Swedish reform pedagogue Ellen Key (1849–1926) and translated into English in 1909, the epistemically heterodox tendencies of a eugenicist anthropotechnics can be found, which mobilize themselves, around 1900, as a social network within the historical *dispositif* of "the breeding of children," or *pediatechnics*. As I will argue below, this eugenicist pediatechnics cannot simply be classified as a single system, but rather as a heterogenous interdiscursive field together with medicine, biology, politics, and pedagogy.

In addition to their connection with a French *anthropotechnie*[217], eugenics as well as pediatechnics are also linked to other fields, since they are applied modes of thought and thereby are more than a simple investigating of theoretical principles. This scientific knowledge was to serve as the practical basis for social optimization. In this sense, Key's popular social pedagogy draws upon various disciplines such as literature, philosophy, medicine, biology, and sociology, and gropes toward – in a manner that was atypical of the traditional pedagogy we found in Kant and

---

[216] Nietzsche, KSA 4, 255; *Thus Spoke Zarathustra*, 95. This quotation from Nietzsche's *Zarathustra* is taken by Ellen Key not by chance from the chapter "On the Land of Education", which deals with newly set values and a spiritual nobility that Zarathustra wants to evoke (Ellen Key, *The Century of the Child*, trans. Marie Franzos, New York/London 1909).

[217] Liggieri, *"Anthropotechnik"*, 63–128.

Humboldt – the theories of heredity. The anthropotechnical principle of breeding that underpins her sociology is "scientific", as the term is widely understood today. What early modern thinkers like Campanella or Thomas More (1478–1535) found in literary utopias now takes place in hospitals, doctors' offices, law books, and laboratories. Breeding now draws closer to an artificial reproduction, connecting herds and societies. Key's conceptual language accordingly focuses on the "fundamental biopolitical structure of modernity", that is "the decision on the value (or nonvalue) of life as such", whereby the body, which is at once a given and a product, and whose health is both a condition and a task, moves to the center of discourse as an experimental object.[218]

A first step is the discernment of the discourses (besides *pediatechnics*) that made possible and influenced the highly consequential reform movement at the dawn of the 20th century. Second, Key's polyvalent concept of a social pedagogy will be examined in more detail. I will thereby attempt to answer questions about discourses of problematization concerning her writing, that is, how Key's "new ethics" positions itself between praxis and theory; in which networks of knowledge (between the breeding of animals and the breeding of humans) are (rhetorically) adapted to one another; and how the rational-Enlightenment discourses of humanism inscribe themselves into a pediatechnical image of man. In closing, we must answer the question of how the cognitive anthropologies of the Enlightenment (after Kant and Humboldt) resulted in a 'backslide' into a naturalistic politics of the body at the end of the 19th century.

With Key and her popular medical-eugenicist way of thinking as a catalyst, another way of approaching the dominant "either/or" between Enlightenment (*education*) and eugenics (*breeding*) emerges. Instead of claiming that one replaced the other, we may speak instead of a transcription (as an over-writing or a rewriting) that can be carried out due to the creation of new media and cultural technologies in which the episteme "man" is interpreted in a more biological and materialistic fashion. A discursive knowledge of man thus generates, circulates, and is passed down through modes of reading taken from the natural sciences. Educational and eugenicist intervention consequently act – and this may sound controversial or provocative – using the same system of coordinates as an anthropotechnics. The concept of anthropotechnics and its implementation as a pediate-

---

[218] Agamben, *Homo Sacer*, 137.

48

chnics, an anthropotechnical pedagogy, that, to put it succinctly, combines education and breeding in order to carry out an (outside) intervention into man is marked above all by planning, organization, and rationality in its attempts to "improve" man's deficient disposition.

2. The Key to Key: Historical and Political Discourses of a "Social Hygiene"

Before turning to an examination of Key's text, we must first look at some examples of the discourse on which Key's main work, *The Century of the Child*, draws, because in this way late 19th- and early 20th-century eugenicist and anthropotechnical tendencies can be elucidated. A social Darwinism then emerges that finds a practical application in the realm of medical-hygienic on the one hand, and on the other is projected in the 'between' of a breeding of individuals, animals (zootechnics/anthropotechnics) and children (pediatechnics). Often semantic concepts and methods are taken from the natural sciences (zoology, for example), while political concerns are borrowed and transcribed into pedagogical discourse. What must be remembered here is that the structures of the rational sciences modify the structures of thinking about pedagogy, so that the body, as a zone of application, comes back into view.

Two important figures in the reception of social Darwinism are Ernst Haeckel (1834–1919), who made Darwin's work well-known in Germany, and the founder of eugenics, Francis Galton (1822–1911). Both men paved the way for Key's thinking during the last third of the 19th century, by defining man as a higher power who not only can but *must* artificially interfere with the evolutionary process. "Nature," according to Galton, "teems with latent life, which man has large powers of evoking under the forms and to the extent which he desires."[219] According to Galton, man has been given the power to direct, which he must transform into a positive eugenics: "We may not be able to create, but we can guide. The processes of evolution are constantly and spontaneously active, some tend towards the bad, some tend towards the good. Our part is to watch for opportunities to *intervene* by checking the former processes and giving free play to the latter."[220] Using

---

[219] Francis Galton, *Hereditary Genius: An Inquiry Into Its Laws and Consequences*, London 1892, 360. Cf. Müller-Wille and Rheinberger, *A Cultural History of Heredity*, 12–13
[220] Ibid., XXVII. Cf. Daniel J. Kevles, *In the Name of Eugenics: Genetics and the Uses of Human Heredity*, New York 1985, Chapter 1.

this same reasoning, the German physician Alfred Ploetz (1860–1940), a contemporary of Key's and a founder of *Rassenhygiene* in Germany, pleads for a systematic reproduction by permitting marriage only between those with healthy genes as well as by selection and the exclusion of the weak and poorly formed.[221] Five years later, Key adds her thoughts to this eugenicist discourse, in which breeding is understood as an improvement of the individual (in her case, the child) and the improvement of the "race".

The rendering scientific of sociology, which also guides Key's pediatechnics, took place at the end of the 19th century. In 1894, homeopathy and medicine were united by the German doctor Heinrich Lahmann (1860–1905), who laid down various criteria for a healthy life: "Air, light, water, sustenance, movement, and rest."[222] With these dietetic "life stimulants" ("Lebensreize") of a bourgeois "hygiene," which notion, as it used by Key and other thinkers, can be defined in the broadest sense of the word, we encounter once again the theme that man must train himself. According to Lahmann, health, humanity, and healthy races are produced by means of corporal optimization techniques. The ideal image of the body is drawn from the heroic stylizations of antiquity. The nationalist public advocate and pioneer of *Freikörperkultur* (Free Body Culture, FKK), Heinrich Pudor (1865–1943), speaks in 1902 of the modern longing for a "lost health", that is, "the naïve health" of the "child-like Greeks."[223] The 18th-century humanist fascination with the ancient Greeks (as seen in Humboldt) is reduced, through the contemporary medical-hygienic interpretation, to the body and its health. Here hygiene is a "form of self-prescribed and self-controlled temperance, a conscious, self-directed attempt to remain 'in balance.'"[224] Following the argument of the historian Phillip Sarasin, we might add that the "aesthetics of existence" that Michel Foucault locates in antiquity also manifested themselves in a hygienic "care of the self"

---

[221] Alfred Ploetz, *Die Tüchtigkeit unserer Rasse und der Schutz der Schwachen. Ein Versuch über Rassenhygiene und ihr Verhältnis zu den humanen Idealen, besonders zum Socialismus. Grundlinien einer Rassen-Hygiene, 1. Theil*, Berlin 1895, 145ff.

[222] Heinrich Lahmann, *Die diätische Blutmischung (Dysämie) als Grundursache aller Krankheiten. Ein Beitrag zur Lehre von der Krankheitsdisposition und Krankheitsverhütung*, Leipzig 1894, 20.

[223] Heinrich Pudor, *Die neue Erziehung. Essays über die Erziehung zur Kunst und zum Leben*, Leipzig 1902, 54.

[224] Philipp Sarasin, "Foucault, Burckhard, Nietzsche und die Hygieniker", in Jürgen Martuschkat (Ed.), *Geschichte schreiben mit Foucault*, Frankfurt a.M./New York 2002, 195–218, p. 200.

(*souci de soi*) in the 19th century.[225] Two currents were expanded in this hygienic *souci de soi* implemented as individual hygiene in the 18th century: first, that of "public hygiene," which was directed toward the body politic, a body that, in distinction to collective humanity (as in Kant and Humboldt) is entirely biological; and secondly an expansion took place through the rise of bacteriology in the 1880s.[226] As a result, a trend develops from about 1900 towards the reform of life itself, which expands into a dietetic and hygienic maxim of health. Pudor formulates this shift clearly and distinctly: it is now one's "duty to be healthy".[227] Every institution, organization, and debate is now directed towards this dietary culture, in which biological procreative health as well as the concept of "race" are foregrounded. It is in this context that the nationalist thinker of the life-reform movement, and the forerunner of the FKK movement in Germany, Richard Ungewitter (1869–1958), defines health as the "flawless functioning of the metabolism in every organ" and sickness *ex negative* as "the opposite".[228] When health becomes compulsory and sickness becomes a stigma, what emerges is the asymmetrical coding of lives as *worthy* or *unworthy*. Research from around 1900 tends to focus more and more on mandatory health and the annihilation of the sickly "other". In the eugenics and *Rassenhygiene* founded by Ploetz, a movement that sets out to improve genes is also and necessarily a political movement. Ploetz, who himself undertook bacterial experiments with frogs, argues for euthanasia with the justification that "if no more weak people were produced, they would no longer need to be eradicated."[229] At the center of this mode of thinking stands "physical life", whereby "race" (in contrast to the bourgeois hygiene of the individual) serves as the starting point for a politics of the body. There are many other eugenicist theorists who could also be mentioned here along with Ploetz, for example, the dermatologist and urologist Hermann Rohleder (1866–1934), who spoke in 1911 of the "pro-

---

[225] Ibid., 207.

[226] Philipp Sarasin, "Die Geschichte der Gesundheitsvorsorge. Das Verhältnis von Selbstsorge und staatlicher Intervention im 19. und 20. Jahrhundert", *Cardiovascular Medicine* 14/2 (2011), 41–45, pp. 42–43.

[227] Pudor, *Die neue Erziehung*, 20.

[228] Richard Ungewitter, *Kultur und Nacktheit. Eine Forderung von Richard Ungewitter*, Stuttgart 1911, 121.

[229] Ploetz, *Die Tüchtigkeit unserer Rasse und der Schutz der Schwachen*, 136.

duction of healthier, stronger progeny."[230] Rohleder extends the concept of "sickness" to genes themselves, when he talks about "sickly gametes" or "sickly processes of reproduction".[231] According to Rohleder and Ploetz, these sickly gametes can produce a "pathological heredity".[232] When cells are defined as "sick," then the notion of biopolitical contamination is not far off. For Rohleder, the goal is not only the promotion of "good" biological material, but also a cordoning off of "bad", worthless material and, as a final step, its elimination. Accordingly, in 1915, he argued for the passage of a law (modeled on similar legislation in the United States, where the first law mandating sterilization was passed in Indiana in 1907) that would sterilize alcoholics, deaf-mutes, the mentally ill, criminals, and other "undesirables".[233] He thought that sterilization was "an appropriate process by means of which a portion of the population could be deterred from reproducing, and thus prevented from passing on their sicknesses."[234]

What we can see from these brief citations from the turn of the 20th century is that, from its very beginnings, the notion of biological heredity was neither neutral nor apolitical, but rather stood in a field of interlocking tensions between discursive practices. It can thus be understood as a "biopolitical dispositive".[235] The practice of *breeding humans*, anthropotechnics – man is primarily an animal according to Galton and other followers – appropriates methods and semantics from zootechnics, that then extend past the level of pure discourse and threaten to become practical in the applied natural science of breeding children, as will be shown in the next chapter.

---

[230] Hermann Rohleder, *Die Zeugung beim Menschen. Eine sexualpathologische Studie aus der Praxis. Mit Anhang: Die künstliche Zeugung (Befruchtung) beim Menschen*, Leipzig 1911, 3.

[231] Ibid., 192ff.

[232] Ibid.

[233] Rohleder, "Der heutige Stand der Eugenik", in *Zeitschrift für Sexualwissenschaften* 2 (1915), 17–28, p. 22.

[234] Florenze Vienne, "Gestörtes Zeugungsvermögen: Samenzellen als neues humanmedizinisches Objekt, 1895–1945", in Florenze Vienne and Christina Brandt (Ed.), *Wissensobjekt Mensch*, 165–187, p. 178.

[235] Müller-Wille and Rheinberger, *A Cultural History of Heredity*, 12. Cf. Maurizio Meloni, *Political Biology: Science and Social Values in Human Heredity from Eugenics to Epigenetics*, New York 2012, 44.

3. From Anthropotechnics to Pediatechnics

Since the Middle Ages there has been a wealth of literature on the breeding of animals and plants, in which breeders, sometimes frequently and sometimes rarely, undertook planned experiments. Over the course of the 18th century, this literature instructed its readers in a particular vocabulary, which also found a more general acceptance among the public. Botanical and zoological experiments nonetheless ran up against their limit when they encountered "man." Attempts at breeding human beings were limited to observations ("feral children," ethnographic studies) and utopian literary speculations (like Campanella's *City of the Sun*).

It is widely known that the intervention into the human (carried out by pedagogy) during the 18th-century Enlightenment took on philosophical and social features (see Rousseau, Kant, Humboldt in this regard). Sloterdijk correctly notes that, in this respect, pedagogy tells the shared history of children and animals.[236] This a completely different kind of intervention into humanity, distinct from all the well-known German metaphors for education in Goethe's "morphology of plants", the development of which culminates in Darwin's and in Galton's works (that is, in evolutionary and eugenicist theories). This distinct intervention thus requires further elucidation.

The 19th century brought forth new technologies of breeding, as well as a series of associations promoting breeding (and breeding registries). According to the historians of science Hans-Jörg Rheinberger and Staffan Müller-Wille, the genealogies and tables published in periodicals devoted to plant and animal breeding were strongly oriented towards strategies in family planning, especially in the middle of the 19th century.[237]

In this epistemic space were, on the one hand, the above-mentioned versions of Galton, Ploetz, Rohleder, etc., and on the other hand, the practitioners of a pedagogy based on the natural sciences (*pediatechnics*).[238] This historical epistemic terrain constitutes the condition for the possibility of a specific way of intervening into childhood education that, from

---

[236] Sloterdijk, *Du mußt dein Leben ändern*, 311; *You must change your life*, 198

[237] Müller-Wille and Rheinberger, *A Cultural History of Heredity*, 135.

[238] It should be clear (and the German context, in which these animal analogies were still fought against with some hostility by strongly held educational humanism, is only one example) that Darwin was not the first (and only) thinker to connect nature breeding with culture breeding (in England similar analogies are presented by Charles Lyell, John Sebright, and William Whewell).

around 1900, consolidated into a science with many far-reaching (practical) possibilities.

What becomes clear in the present analysis is that, from the middle of the 19th century onwards, various sciences acted in an interdisciplinary fashion. Besides medicine, philosophy, psychology, law, politics, and biology, pedagogy too was caught in the net of anthropotechnics. Breeding and Education move together within these epistemic coordinates, as the child becomes an experimental object that can be measured, investigated, and illuminated. The doctor Johann Baptist Ullersperger (1798–1878) can be regarded as an early example of this interdisciplinary nexus. In the pedagogical–medicinal *Journal for Pediatric Illness* in 1867 – that is, at that time when the French anthropotechnical discourse was developing – he had proclaimed that "zootechnics is in fact more developed than anthropotechnics, which latter discipline triggers the education of children."[239] The potent "parallelism" between "husbandry" and the "breeding of humans" thus lies in the foreground of pediatechnics, because "the sophisticated practitioners of animal husbandry know perfectly well what to do in order to improve a race; here we need only look to Spain and to England – much less concern is shown, however, for the improvement of the human race."[240] Ullersperger's investigations bring praxis (a praxis directed towards the goal of a "healthy" life) increasingly into the foreground of these considerations. Not only does Ullersperger offer a diagnosis of his time, but he himself is a symptom of it, because around 1830 medicine began to modernize itself, basing its knowledge on empirical experimentation. The doctor's mere experience of life no longer suffices. Experimental knowledge was needed, a knowledge that could be taken from zootechnics, among other sources. We can see just how far these arguments spread if we turn to Galton in 1865. The father of "eugenics" writes in the same vein as the aforementioned authors when he says that "[i]f a twentieth part of the cost and pains were spent in measures for the improvement of the

---

[239] Johann Baptist Ullersperger, "Pädiotrophie, Pädiopathieen und Pädiatrik im Allgemeinen und in ihrem richtigen Verhältnisse zur Morbilität und Mortalität der Neugeborenen, der Säuglinge und der Kinder in den ersten Lebensjahren", *Journal für Kinderkrankheiten*, ed. Friedrich Jacob Behrend 49 (1867), 1–132, p. 40.
[240] Ibid.

human race that is spent on the improvement of the breed of horses and cattle, what a galaxy of genius might we not create!"[241]

At the start of the 20th century, the idea of a biosocial "pediatechnics", applied emphatically as a praxis though nonetheless heavily theorized, became an analogue to an applied anthropotechnics, which already enjoyed academic legitimacy and which was socially accepted. At this time, the concept of "pediatechnics" designated "a science with the child as its practical goal", following the Belgian doctor Ovide Decroly's (1871––1932) definitive 1907 formulation.[242] Semantically adjacent concepts were housed within this notion of a pediatechnics. Drawing on "anthropology", "pediology" became a potent term for an empirically grounded, experimental science of the child, with the publication of Oscar Chrisman's *Pediology: Blueprint for a Science of the Child* in 1896.[243] In this text, pediology was given an interdisciplinary scientific basis (in fields like biology, psychology, philosophy, anthropology, etc.), "furnishing the material on which pediology establishes its basis, and lifts itself to the place it is meant to occupy."[244] The influence of this interdisciplinary concept is most clearly perceptible in the *International Congress for Psychology* (1909), in which the applied field of "pediology" received its own section. The practical *dispositif* of "pediology", whose echoes could be heard as far off as Russia, was further divided by the physician Édouard Claparède (who was on the organizing committee for an *International Congress of Pediology* in 1911 with Ernst Meumann, the founder of pedagogical psychology and experimental pedagogy in Germany) into experimental pedagogy, school hygiene, and medical pedagogy. Ernst Meumann, the experimental psychologist, saw experimental psychology as the "spiritual mother"

---

[241] Francis Galton, "Hereditary Talent and Character", *Macmillan's Magazine* 12 (1865), 157–166, 318–327, 165ff.

[242] Ovide Decroly, "Sociètè de Pèdotechnie", *Die Experimentelle Pädagogik. Organ der Arbeitsgemeinschaft für experimentelle Pädagogik mit besonderer Berücksichtigung der experimentellen Didaktik und der Erziehung Schwachbegabter und abnormer Kinder*, ed. Ernst Meumann, Vol. 4 (1907), 255–256.

[243] Oscar Chrisman, *Paidologie. Entwurf zu einer Wissenschaft des Kindes*, Diss. phil. Jena 1896.

[244] Chrisman, *Paidologie*, 9. On the practical "paidological laboratory course", which included anthropometry (or "paidometry", ibid., 39), see Chapter III (ibid., 46ff). In the discourses of the 1910/20s "Paidology" and "Pedology" were often used synonymously and with little differentiation.

of an empirical and experimental research pedagogy.[245] In 1894 he, who regarded experimental pedagogy as "a movement scientifically parallel" to the school reform movement, became the first assistant to Wilhelm Wundt at the Institute for Experimental Psychology.[246] It was Meumann who set down the connection between pedagogy and experimental psychology and who "united in himself these two currents (pure philosophy and experimental psychology)."[247] Through his appointment to a professorship of "philosophy, and in particular psychology" at the Philosophical Seminar and Psychological Laboratory at the University of Hamburg in 1911 (a forerunner of the university founded in 1919), this science received institutional legitimation.

Just as anthropology provided foundational research for the applied science of anthropotechnics, so too pediology was to be the scientific groundwork for an applied pediatechnics.[248]

The gathering and systemization of data on children in an empirical research into childhood was attempted in pediology in order to ensure that this discipline, as a field of praxis (namely, as pediatechnics), could optimally map the object of its investigation. This reconfiguration of quality into quantity posed a social question: which models of education and instruction (the most efficient and rational organization of a class) produced the best citizens? Rationalization and increased efficiency in the instructed thus acted as a normalizing and "homogenizing" force whereby the "abnormal" was shunted out of the classroom and labelled a disruptive element.[249] Thus, in a wave of euphoria, pedagogues were styled as a cross between politicians and scientists, while the science of pediology

---

[245] Ernst Meumann, "Experimentelle Pädagogik und Schulreform", *Zeitschrift für Pädagogische Psychologie* 12 (1911), 1–13, p. 1; Meumann, *Vorlesungen zur Einführung in die Experimentelle Pädagogik und ihre psychologischen Grundlagen* (Vol. 1, second edition), Leipzig 1911, 2, quoted from Paul Probst and Wolfgang G. Bringmann, "Ernst Meumann and William Stern: Analyse ihres Wirkens in Hamburg (1910–1933) unter Berücksichtigung biographischer und soziokultureller Hintergründe", *Geschichte der Psychologie* 19 (1993), 1–14, p. 6.

[246] Ibid.

[247] Staatsarchiv Hamburg, *Hochschulwesen, Personalakte E. Meumann, Dozenten- und Personalakten* I 47, quoted from Probst and Bringmann, "Ernst Meumann und William Stern", 7.

[248] For a detailed study, please refer to Marc Depaepe, *Zum Wohl des Kindes?: Pädologie, pädagogische Psychologie und experimentelle Pädagogik in Europa und den USA. 1890–1940*, Weinheim 1993, 173.

[249] Ibid., 172.

promoted itself as a medical discipline devoted to improving the nation, with the "biological and sociological dimensions of education [receiving] particular attention."[250] The social questions of pediology became biosocial, while schools and classrooms became, as the Belgian scholar of education Marc Depaepe noted in his study of pediology, "the actual fabric of pediatechnics."[251] This is because through various interventions (like systematic medical oversight, or the introduction of compulsory medical investigations, for example, before a marriage license could be granted) man attempted to maintain or to produce a "normal heredity", in the words of the Belgian eugenicist Louis Querton in 1912.[252]

The very title of the periodical *Experimental Pedagogy* evinces the science's programmatic affinity with an educational technology that had the underpinnings of a natural science. Just as in Ullersperger's article for the *Journal for Pediatric Illnesses* (1867), here too the child is the perfect object of experimentation: if one wants to change society right down to its very roots, that is to, be *radical* in the most literal sense of the word, one must start with the child. In the fourth volume of the periodical, published in 1908 and edited by Meumann, the breeding ideas of Decroly, later the professor of hygiene, can be found. The experimental process of anthropotechnics is there terminologically as well as methodologically transferred to the field of pedagogy (*pediatechnics*):

> For a long time now, scientific interests have known how to turn the breeding of animals into an actual science: zootechnics. Recently those who collect concepts have given the name *anthropotechnicist* to those who concern themselves with the life of man – whether as an individual or a social being – and who, in this monstrous realm, search for the means to produce a better development in humanity. Just as pedology is a branch of anthropology, so pedotechnics is a branch of anthro-

---

[250] Ibid., 173; on the zeitgeist see Nicolas Smelten, "Pédotechnie", *Zuid en Noord* 1 (1910), 110–113; and Alexis Sluys, *L'Evolution de la pédagogie*, Geneva 1911.

[251] Depaepe, *Zum Wohl des Kindes?*, 178. "Factory" and "technical access" seemed to be connected here more than simply in their visual language; rather, a special rational access to the optimization of the child becomes apparent.

[252] Louis Querton, "L'Organisation du controle du développement de l'enfant", *Ioteyko* 2 (1912), 105–111, p. 105, quoted from Depaepe, *Zum Wohl des Kindes?*, 174.

potechnics. It represents the science of the child for a practical purpose.[253]

This article makes clear the significance of the social connection for pediatechnics ("Society of Pediatechnics"). This discipline had an important research center in Brussels and it was concerned above all with "complete care" for the child, even before birth. Decroly held that it was absolutely necessary to create a new word for this discipline, namely "pediatechnics", a term that is both "more expressive and suggestive" than the traditional word "pedagogy," which is largely limited by its "common usage."[254] Pediatechnics thus became a programmatic byword, as had anthropotechnics.

What is noteworthy here is that at the first (and last) *International Congress for Pediology* (in Brussels in 1911) the subject of school hygiene (in the broadest sense of the word, even the "ideal" school bench was discussed here) took precedence over the other sections.[255] For Arthur Nyns, the chair of the Belgian Union for Pediatechnics, pediatechnics was concerned with "hygiene, with reproduction, with care for infants, with rational methods of teaching, in short, with fitting the individual to the surroundings in which he must live. It is also meant to investigate the genetic and social factors that influence the child's development, positively as well as negatively."[256] This "fitting" sounds like a liberal educational-philosophical conception. However, it focuses – like its terminological starting point, anthropotechnics – on biopolitical interventions that were again relevant to the biological and hygienic worldview.

The reciprocal relationship between "sociology and biology" thus determined the tenor of many anthropotechnical (as well as pediatechnical) texts of this time and established the term in the discursive as well as the academic landscape.[257] And so, from 1891 to 1914, 21 periodicals across the world were devoted to child psychology (six alone in Germany), while

---

[253] Decroly, "Société de Pédotechnie", 256.

[254] Ibid.

[255] Marc Depaepe, Frank Simon, Frederik Herman, and Angelo Van Gorp, "Brodskys hygienische Klappschulbank: Zu leicht für die schulische Mentalität", in Karin Priem, Gudrun M. König, and Rita Casale (Ed.), *Zeitschrift für Pädagogik, 58. Beiheft: Die Materialität der Erziehung: Kulturelle und soziale Aspekte pädagogischer Objekte*, Weinheim 2012, 50–65, p. 57.

[256] Arthur Nyns, "La pédotechnie", *Zuid en Noord* 1 (1910), 469–482, p. 474, quoted from Depaepe, *Zum Wohl des Kindes?*, 173.

[257] Decroly, "Société de Pédotechnie", 255.

four institutes unattached to any university conducted research into experimental pedagogy as well as psychology.[258] William Stern, who in 1918 had already reflected on these positivistic currents, observed that the school was often regarded as "an active instrument that is potentially unlimited in its capacity to sculpt human beings."[259] In this way of looking at things, the human (*ánthrōpos*) – and the child (*páis*) – is a material to be formed, a material that only needed the appropriate technology (and technology is understood here both an as ability and as rational material technologies such as chairs, rooms, and benches) in order to form and optimally model a person.

4. Ellen Key's Century of the Child

What becomes clear in the preceding discussion is that, around 1900, the *Zeitgeist*, nourished by 40 years of social Darwinism, as well by the analogy between humans and animals, began to implement changes by working on the body, as well as on "life", and no longer on human consciousness. It is significant in this regard that at the turn of the 20th century there was a "rediscovery" of Mendel's law in at least three respects.[260] This "rediscovery" of heredity was of particular importance for pedagogy, because now one could argue more credibly against the optimizing influence of education, improved quality of life, and medical therapy. Breeding as an intervention "on" as well as "in' the body gains the upper hand over education. Ploetz expresses these thoughts in 1895 in his *The Proficiency of Our Race (Die Tüchtigkeit unserer Rasse)*: "Outward impressions, education, and functional training can only unfold given traits to a certain point, so that they can function better for the individual in question. But the bolstering of positive faculties in the genetics of the next generation,

---

[258] Helga Kelle, "Kinder in der Schule. Zum Zusammenhang von Schuldpädagogik und Kindheitsforschung", in Georg Breidenstein and Annedore Prengel (Ed), *Schulforschung und Kindheitsforschung – Ein Gegensatz*, Wiesbaden 2005, 139–160, p. 141.

[259] William Stern, *Person und Sache. System des kritischen Personalismus. Zweiter Band: Die menschliche Persönlichkeit*, Leipzig 1918, 180.

[260] For the simultaneous discovery see Hugo De Vries, *Das Spaltungsgesetz der Bastarde* (March 14, 1900), Carl Correns, *Gregor Mendel's Regel über das Verhalten der Nachkommenschaft der Rassenbastarde* (April 24, 1900), Erich von Tschermak-Seyenegg, *Über künstliche Kreuzung bei pisum sativum* (June 2, 1900). Cf. Hans-Jörg Rheinberger, *An Epistemology of the Concrete: Twentieth-Century Histories of Life*, Durham/London 2010, 79.

that is, actually increasing the capital of the human capacity for happiness is a problem of species-life and, as a result, falls entirely into the realm of *Rassenhygiene*."[261] For anthropotechnics and pediatechnics, the humanistic program of education has, in a sense, failed, because "education only fine-tunes breeding, but cannot entirely replace it."[262] This means that if man is to be transformed, then the transformation must take place *beneath* his skin. The knowledge of man required for an immediate intervention is reduced to a knowledge of the body. The measure of "life" is thus politicized, so that it is no longer the free man, with his individual qualities, but rather the *corpus* that constitutes the new subject of politics *(polis)* and that constitutes the new national body. Following Sarasin, what is now foregrounded in this discourse is no longer a concern about damaging the individual's nerves with individual acts of sexual intercourse or the individual's learning to master his drives, but rather the scientist's taking responsibility for the health of the race by preventing poor genetic inheritance.[263] In addition to this politicizing of biological life, a Nietzschean "aestheticization" also takes place: life itself becomes a malleable artwork such that man can make "his own being into an artwork."[264]

Key's work can be said to stand at the outset of this phase of the conceptualization of pediatechnics, in that she adapts this medical-eugenicist discourse in and for her new pedagogy and ethics. In her view, her book *The Century of the Child* marks a breakthrough into a new discourse of the body ("the holiness of generation").[265] The Swedish reform pedagogue had her finger on the pulse of her time and saw her ideas circulate throughout her world. The poet Rainer Marie Rilke, in a review for a June 1902 edition of the *Bremer Tageblatt und General-Anzeiger*, almost prophetically remarked: "And this book, in a penetrating and loving way, is an experience, a document that one will not be able to brush off easily. In the course of this century, which has just begun, readers will return to this book again and again. It will be cited, refuted, relied upon and attacked;

---

[261] Ploetz, *Die Tüchtigkeit unserer Rasse*, 13.

[262] Oswald Spengler, *Der Untergang des Abendlandes*, München 1923, 967.

[263] Sarasin, *Reizbare Maschinen – eine Geschichte des Körpers 1765–1914*, Frankfurt a. M. 2001, 445.

[264] Ellen Key, in Wilhelm Flitner and Gerhard Kudritzki (Ed.), *Die Deutsche Reformpädagogik. Band I: Die Pioniere der pädagogischen Bewegung*, Düsseldorf/München 1961, 63.

[265] Key, *The Century of the Child*, 3.

in any case, one will have to deal with it."[266] With her unique style, which mixes the religious with the mystical as well as the medical, Key paints a picture of a new and healthier race, whose harbinger is the child. For Key, a careful reader of Nietzsche who had understood man as engaged "in the process of becoming", it is possible to intervene into man in order to modify him.[267] Since man's body is not static and does not exist beyond the scope of time, it offers the possibility of "so influencing his future development that a higher type of man will be produced."[268] Building on the traditional discourse of anthropotechnics, Key draws parallels between man and the world of animals and plants, upon which man had already exerted his "will" in breeding.[269] Thus, in Key's biopolitics, man can be described as "an animal whose politics places his existence as a living being in question."[270] Under no circumstances can the "ennobling of the human race" be left to "chance" in this game.[271] The natural sciences provide a reference point for a program of breeding, since "it will take the thorough influence of the scientific view of humanity to restore the full naïve conviction, belonging to the ancient world, of the significance of the body."[272] Thanks to scientific progress, it is now possible to return to the "pure" organism, because, according to Key, the body can now be detached from Christianity, which had damned it. Key also criticizes the sacrament of marriage using the same reasoning. On the other hand, she pronounces the body itself to be "holy": neither the spirit nor consciousness are paramount, but rather the body, which is sacred. It is the body that produces, that loves, that lives. Partners do not have to marry and do not have to remain faithful to one another so long as they care for their bodies, for their "purity", and for their hygiene. Paradoxically, the body has a double nature: on the one hand, it is the malleable, material, experimental object of the sciences; on the other hand it is also something sacred and closely guarded in a world that has become godless, in the loose sense of Nietzsche's dictum that "God is dead". However, it is in no sense untouchable. Or, as Käte Mayer-Drawe

---

[266] Rainer-Maria Rilke, "Das Jahrhundert des Kindes" (1902), *Bremer Tageblatt und General-Anzeiger*, (4) 132, 8. June 1902, in Rilke, *Sämtliche Werke*, Vol. 5, Wiesbaden/Frankfurt a. M. 1955–1966, 584ff.

[267] Key, *The Century of the Child*, 3.

[268] Ibid., 5.

[269] Ibid.

[270] Foucault, *The History of Sexuality 1*, 143.

[271] Key, *The Century of the Child*, 5.

[272] Ibid., 5–6.

puts it: "[Pedagogy] venerates the child as a messiah, and surveys him as an object among other objects."[273] Key gives a scientific foundation to her notion of a "self-purification" in order to lend it more substance. In so doing she focused, like other well-known thinkers including Darwin and Malthus, on what she calls "the significance of selection and the danger of degeneration".[274] Key goes on to mention August Weismann, Alfred Russel Wallace, Galton, and Herbert Spencer. One must "on the basis of natural science attain, in a newer and more noble form, the whole antique love for bodily strength and beauty, the whole antique reverence for the divine character of the continuation of the race; combined with the whole modern consciousness of the soulful happiness of ideal love!"[275]

First and foremost, the manner in which Key, the reform pedagogue, blurs the line between, on the one hand, the ethics of antiquity and the discourses of the body, and, on the other, the modern natural sciences, can be questioned. Nonetheless, Key's readings of these discourses are marked by her desire, first, to codify pedagogy as a fixed science and, second, to carry out an intervention into man using this new pedagogy, which sets little store by the model of education. Pedagogy is no longer concerned with the history of education, but rather with popularizing knowledge and inventing laws that might contribute to the child's improved biological 'formation' (now in the concrete and biological sense). "The notion of perfectibility no longer serves the individual in developing all of his forces to completion," according to Meyer-Drawe, "as in the strain of thought that follows Rousseau. Instead, perfectibility now serves the genus."[276] Pedagogy now becomes a subcategory of the natural sciences and, with Key, becomes *pediatechnics*. In her biological codification of the social, the reform pedagogue's attack on marriage is not an end in itself, but is rather meant to be the basis of a "new ethic" in which an extramarital affair can no longer be called "immoral".[277] Only those actions, practices, and genes that "give occasion to a weak offspring, and produces bad conditions for the development of their offspring" should be called immoral.[278] Morality is *embodied*

---

[273] Käte Meyer-Drawe, *Diskurse des Lernens*, Paderborn 2012, 63.

[274] Key, *The Century of the Child*, 12.

[275] Ibid., 12.

[276] Käte Meyer-Drawe, "Töten aus Barmherzigkeit? Biopolitische Tendenzen der Lebensreformbewegung. Erich Christian Schröder zum 80. Geburtstag", in Käte Meyer-Drawe and Kristin Platt (Ed.), *Wissenschaft im Einsatz*, München 2007, 205–217.

[277] Key, *The Century of the Child*, 13–14.

[278] Ibid.

and the new "religious dogma" follows the religion of eugenics.[279] Key agrees entirely with Galton when she writes that "[...] the Ten Commandments on this subject will not be written by the founders of religion, but by scientists."[280] With this return to the primacy of the natural sciences as a means for setting values for life, and as a substitute for the old religion (Christianity) that is hostile to life, Key's poetic style claims to be grounded in a scientific argument that is meant to convince and dazzle a wider readership. For that reason she swathes bodies with statistics from pathology as when, for example, she shows that "of three hundred idiots, one hundred and forty-five had alcoholic parents. Epilepsy, too, is often produced by the same cause."[281] Based on this data, in order to enforce a norm as well as a healthy social body, she demands "medical testimony before marriage."[282] An anthropological praxis is to follow from this anthropological science. The doctor who looks *into* man, into man's genetic material, is thereby the authority who must answer for the success or failure of a higher breeding. The place of the monarch has been taken by that of the scientist, who now decides whether each life is worthy or unworthy.[283]

In Key's view not only does Christianity pose problems as far as marriage is concerned, but its emphasis on "pity" and "mercy" towards the weak and sickly also stand in the way of the larger goal of species health. "Heathen society in its hardness exposed weak or crippled children. Christian society on the other hand, has gone so far in its mildness, that it prolongs the life of the child who is incurably ill, physically and psychically, even if he is misshapen and so becomes an hourly torment to himself and his surroundings."[284] Key's biopolitics was not only guided by the "right to die", but also by a discourse of optimizing life.[285] The central role is assigned to the concept of worthiness. Medicine becomes an economy because it must gauge "how much" the biological body of the individual is worth, and whether it is damaging to (understood as causing a loss of value in) 'the biological body of the *Volk*' ('Volkskörper'). Thus, according to Key, the individual must keep to the mechanisms prescribed for the devel-

---

[279] Francis Galton, "Eugenics: Its definition, scope, and hope", *The American Journal of Sociology*, 1/10 (1904), 43–51, p. 43.

[280] Key, *The Century of the Child*, 14.

[281] Ibid., 24.

[282] Ibid.

[283] Cf. Agamben, *Homo Sacer*, 122.

[284] Key, *The Century of the Child*, 33.

[285] Foucault, *The History of Sexuality 1*, 139.

opment of life, wherein individual moral actions represent a risk to "a continuously progressing optimization of life."[286] Since the eugenicist calculus is clearly an economical one, the philosophers Michael Hardt and Antonio Negri go so far as to postulate that productive forces are in actual fact completely "biopolitical": they traverse and cross not only production but also the entire sphere of reproduction.[287] Through the synthesis of the systems of economics and science, man himself becomes a commodity and life itself becomes a form of capital: biopolitics becomes bioeconomics. The sickly person must die so that the healthy person can live efficiently. "Only when death is inflicted through compassion, will the humanity of the future show itself in such a way, that the doctor under control and responsibility can painlessly extinguish such suffering."[288] In true social Darwinist fashion, Key applies the pathos of pity to separate the sick from the healthy, since in a biopolitics one is able "to put to death legally those who pose a kind of biological danger to others."[289] However, even Key knows that the doctor and the government could never bring about a change in the thinking of the larger population on their own. It is only from this change that a new mode of action might come into being. Key thus once again takes up the theme of man and his individual hygiene as well as his moral disposition. Making reference to the title of her text, *The Century of Child*, she speaks of the "obligation" that parents feel "to every child."[290] The child serves first as "a focal point at which the health of the parents is bound up with that of their children, [...],"[291] and secondly, as Schroder says in 1894, echoing Key, "as a photograph of the parents in the act of reproduction."[292] In the child one can find, as if by hermeneutics, the defects of the parents. The *natural* child is thus both "a biological fact and a task".[293] It functions as the guarantor of the race. Stimulated by medical-eugenicist research, Key develops a new ethics for couples, free of Christianity. This ethics dictates maxims of practical action and it is therefore meant to bring about a "complete revolution in [the] theory of value."[294]

---

[286] Thomas Lemke, *Gouvernementalität und Biopolitik*, Wiesbaden 2007, 126.

[287] Michael Hardt and Antonio Negri, *Empire*, Cambridge (MA) 2000, 390.

[288] Key, *The Century of the Child*, 33.

[289] Foucault, *The History of Sexuality 1*, 138.

[290] Key, *The Century of the Child*, 33.

[291] Sarasin, *Reizbare Maschinen*, 434.

[292] H. Schroeder, *Die Gesunderhaltung in der Ehe*, 5. Ed., Leipzig 1984, 61.

[293] Meyer-Drawe, "Töten aus Barmherzigkeit?", 214ff.

[294] Key, *The Century of the Child*, 156.

In light of what we have teased out here, it can be seen that Key's text runs parallel to the discourse of anthropotechnics. As a heterogenous hybrid entity, it borrows from various disciplines with the goal of developing a praxis that intervenes into man. Its rhetoric draws on quasi-religious rites as well as on Kant's technology of duty. It only *seems* to be the case that a deep intellectual-historical gulf separates her from Enlightenment philosophers like Kant and Humboldt, whose tradition she nonetheless follows. Kant and Humboldt too base their respective notions of education [*Erziehung*] and self-cultivation [*Bildung*] on scientific, experimental theories. Both are characterized by the attempt to bring forth a future humanity using planned methods. Nonetheless, for both thinkers these goals focus on the cognitive basis of an anthropology seen from a pragmatic perspective. Key, by contrast, is a social Darwinist. She elevates the natural sciences to the position of a master discipline, a discipline by means of which "plans for civilizing man, and for elevating human race could be carried out."[295] With her biological–pedagogical manifesto she hopes to intervene *into* the body. In the course of this process "the natural sciences, in which must now be numbered psychology, should be the basis of juristic science as well as of pedagogy."[296] The imitation of nature which is part of Humboldt's methodology is the basis for eugenicist laws in Key. In order for her project to be realized and for the measures of selection to be enforced, the reform pedagogue requires the support of the state so that the "human race will be gradually freed from atavisms which reproduce lower and preceding stages of development."[297] The counterproductive application of "social" protection for the sickly and the lame only brings forth negative evolutionary effects in Key's view. The only way out of degeneration into mediocrity lies in a systematically applied selection that is rationally planned and that intervenes in a sensible way into the development of the human race. For the social practitioner – as well as for eugenicist–anthropotechnicist movements as a whole – what is of paramount importance is ensuring the survival of the *Volk*, of the race, or of humanity, which must be continuously "protected" from external "impurities" and illnesses.[298]

---

[295] Ibid., 27.

[296] Ibid., 46.

[297] Ibid.

[298] Otmar von Verschuer, *Rassenhygiene als Wissenschaft und Staatsaufgabe*, Frankfurt a. M. 1936, 5.

In addition to this external compulsion (objective laws), Key believes that human beings function best when they are morally answerable to themselves (subjective basis) and when they follow a technology of duty and a voluntary "*askesis*" and thus refrain from choosing to reproduce with a sickly partner. It is the "duty" of those couples "to abstain from marriage when they know that they have to transmit a bad inheritance unfortunate inheritance to a new generation."[299] Insofar as the individual must subordinate his wishes to those of the body politic, he disappears into the collective and love – or, as Key calls it, "eros" – is no longer directed towards the partner but rather onto the "pure" continuation of the race by means of 'euthanasia'.[300]

We have already mentioned just how emphatically the biological–pedagogical intervention, for Key, has distanced itself from the theories of the educators Kant and Humboldt, at least at first glance. That distance seems even greater when Key draws upon and perverts the Kantian imperative. Here Key is very close to, but also impossibly distant from, being a humanistic educator: "In all these promptings of instinct, in all these categorical imperatives of the nerves and the blood, human beings must be at the same time obedient listeners and strict masters. On this depends the future happiness of love, and with it a happier future race."[301] We must also be attentive to another discourse that resonates here, besides that of Kant's categorical imperative. At this time, "blood" had already lost its significance as "the juice of life" and ceded this place to "sperm".[302] Nonetheless, in Key it is the central factor, since in her thinking it is the focal point of contamination. Blood must be protected from enemies like germs or bad genes. This image of blood had already undergone a historical shift because, in her text, for example, the "concern with genealogy", in the blue-blooded aristocracy, became "a preoccupation with heredity."[303]

---

[299] Key, *The Century of the Child*, 49ff.
[300] Ibid., 12.
[301] Ibid., 57.
[302] Sarasin, "Feind im Blut: Die Bedeutung des Blutes in der deutschen Bakteriologie, 1870–1900", in Christina von Braun (Ed.), *Mythen des Blutes*, Frankfurt a. M. 2007, 296–310, pp. 306, 307.
[303] Foucault, *The History of Sexuality 1*, 124.

6. Education and breeding – On the Interdependence of Enlightenment and Eugenics

In summary, we might say that in Key's text, we find an anthropotechnical and a pediatechnical breeding *par excellence*. This is because, first, in her hygienic imperative she transposes the traditional comparison between human beings and animals onto the child, as well as onto the race, while the myths of evolution (Haeckel, Spencer) are coupled to the newly-formed institutions of public health and welfare. On the other hand, Key's *Century of the Child* is itself a polemic for a new ethics, one that hopes to prepare the way for new interventions into the body. Her pedagogical concern – on account of which she introduces scientific, eugenicist, and philosophical argumentation into her work – is to bring about a change of behavior in the largest possible public. Complex arguments are inevitably banalized in the service of this goal. All of the aforementioned biopolitical discourses that were written for the wider public around 1900 are bundled together in this simplification: the will to a strong, healthy race that can only be formed through the younger generation; the exclusion of the sick; the reference to medical evolutionary theses for support as well as the analogical relationship between human beings and animals. Key's intervention is thus the embodiment of an anthropotechnics of breeding, which attempts "to maintain the psychic force and moral purity of the social body" and to "eradicate the shame of the degenerate and the degenerate parts of the social body."[304]

In spite of this radicality, Key still remains shackled to the coordinates of pedagogy. Hence she speaks of the "amelioration of the human race", a statement that both Kant or Humboldt could have made.[305] The unsettling aspect of Key's thought is that, although she distances herself from the Enlightenment educators in her argumentation and in her biopolitical methods, she nonetheless works within the same epistemic tableau. Her interventions into man are of a physical nature; hence she writes that in some cases, it is correct to "give life", in others "to take it away."[306] To simply leave the matter standing by noting the superficial distinction be-

---

[304] Foucault, *Der Wille zum Wissen. Sexualität und Wahrheit*, Vol. 1, Frankfurt a. M. 1977, 58.

[305] Key, *The Century of the Child*, 59.

[306] Ibid., 60.

tween Kant and Humboldt on the one hand and Key on the other (and by the same token between pedagogy and pediatechnics/anthropotechnics) would be short-sighted, because Key too knows that she must change minds in order to create a new model of physical nature. First, men must "agree to sacrifice the most dangerous of all liberties, giving life to a defective offspring" for that would make the passage of any further laws superfluous.[307] External compulsion (laws for Key, discipline for Kant) fall away and "new ideas of law" are formed once the imperative has been internalized or incorporated.[308]

On the one hand, education and breeding are infinitely far apart from one another. Here *logos*, there *bios*; here cognitive modeling, there physical modeling; here pedagogy, there pediatechnics. On the other hand, both disciplines are sisters in the interdiscursive triangle of *breeding, taming* and *education.*

Education and breeding both make use of compulsion and discipline, both have as their goal the optimization of the (human) race, both are externally oriented towards students or children, and both follow a rational plan – and this is the most difficult and irritating part when one reads a pedagogical text like Key's *Century of the Child* today – both are two sides of the same anthropotechnical coin.

---

[307] Ibid.
[308] Ibid., 33.

III. Anthropoetics – Optimization Discourses in Literature

Anthropotechnics is not only at work in scientific disciplines like education, "*Bildung*" and the natural sciences. It also has a foothold in literary discourses of optimization and models of the human-machine. Literary visions thus define a certain range of possibilities in anthropotechnics. When and which anthropotechnical visions were articulable in literature? The preceding chapters have attempted to demonstrate the history as well as the parameters of an anthropotechnics. These discourses of problematization can be deepened and built up in further analyses, but the present study is also meant to serve as the groundwork for a literary theory. This might appear paradoxical, since literature is often chronologically prior to other discourses and grasps the relations as well as the problematics of human optimization much more deeply. In this sense literature itself seems to be a kind of experiment in which futuristic as well as technological ideas are tried out and evaluated. What I will attempt to do in the second part of this book, which investigates various literary examples, is to show, by way of experiment, the various modalities, frameworks and teleological directions through which anthropotechnical discourses inscribe themselves in literature. It bears repeating that the following is a kind of pilot project and it does not aim to provide any dogmatic interpretations or holistic understandings of the texts discussed. Rather, these readings will retain an experimental character. This analysis will therefore leave itself open to the charge of using the concepts and parameters of anthropotechnics tautologically, since what was worked out in the first part of this study is taken as a starting point. Against such a hypothetical criticism, it might be said that the preceding work covers no new field, but rather opens a new viewpoint on preexisting fields. I will not attempt to read a particular discourse into the literary works discussed in the following, but rather to draw anthropotechnical aspects out of these literary discourses. To what extent this attempt succeeds without forcing the works to conform to this conceptual framework remains for the reader to decide. In this further reflection on "anthropotechnics", I will attempt to expand the concept into the aesthetic realm of literature, thus yielding an "anthropoetics". I will examine the texts from a single standpoint, that of optimization, and will at the same time ignore all other points of access (like verse form, analysis of characters, etc.) of these multi-faceted works. This follows from the aforementioned thematic focus.

In this investigation, literary figures that can be regarded optimization narratives or anthropoetic programs will be analyzed. A further point that can be made here is that the books themselves can be understood as technologies and "machines". So, for example, Deleuze and Guattari treat books as "abstract machines" that can join with other books to produce "machinic assemblages".[309] This notion of a technologization of books (bibliotechnics) as a medium in itself must remain a suggestion, and will not be further explored here.[310]

Literary anthropotechnics, or better, anthropoetics can be divided schematically into two subcategories. Both subcategories, as the study of the three concepts above has shown, constitute a technology applied to human beings.[311]

The first literary–anthropotechnical category describes the optimization of existing humans. Enhancement, which acts on the person from outside, will be placed under that heading. Here the human is passive and is acted on externally. Through cybernetic prostheses, sport, surgery, medication, but also through discipline and training, human performance and

---

[309] Gilles Deleuze and Félix Guattari, *A Thousand Plateaus: Capitalism and Schizophrenia*, trans. Brian Massumi, London 2005, 4.

[310] Donna Haraway also undertakes the mechanization of text and language, since, for her, cyborgs can represent "text, machine, body and metaphor" (Donna Haraway, *Simians, Cyborgs and Women: The Reinvention of Nature*, New York 1991, 212). What man has in common with writing is that he can be copied by means of modern biotechnology: in the beginning was the copy (see Haraway, "The Biopolitics of Postmodern Bodies: Determinations of Self in Immune System Discourse", in Janet Price and Margrit Shildrick (Ed.), *Feminist Theory and the Body: A Reader*, New York 1999, 203–214).

[311] 'Anthropoetics' is an apt term in reference to literature, which I owe to Carsten Zelle. In our understanding of the term, 'anthropoetics' refers to the optimization and production of human beings in literature, *poiesis* or *poetics* is the term for 'creating' as well as for 'literature'.

the human life force increase themselves. This optimization is transferred to the literary subject of the experiment. Faust's rejuvenation (*Faust I*, "Witches' Kitchen") examines this process of experimentation more precisely. These externally applied technologies are contrasted against internally applied technologies. The terms *external* and *internal* and *outside* and *inside* have no metaphysical connotations here, but refer to different praxes. For that matter, when speaking of technologies of the self, we are necessarily speaking of a self that can experience itself. That does not mean, however, that we are in the realm of philosophical idealism. We might note here that "inner" and "outer" can also denote "autopoetic" and "heteropoetic".[312] In any case, these terminologies are further problematized when, in the course of pedagogical reflections, they are applied to the subjective will, since the discipline performed by the institution of the school might not be exclusively heteronomous, as it is "embodied" in the child, while it is far from clear whether a voluntarily chosen enhancement is working from "inside" or "outside". The sociologist Jürgen Straub indicates this indistinctness when he speaks of a "(more or less) heteronomous" or a "(more or less) autonomous" process of optimization.[313] With these considerations in mind, I will make judicious use of the adverbial doublet "outer-inner".

According to Foucault, the *technologies* that take place inside constitute a "care of the self," while according to Sloterdijk technologies of the self are a kind of optimizing "artistry".[314] A literary figure can inwardly direct technologies in order to give shape to his life from the inside out, to improve, or, above all, to aestheticize. We will turn to Friedrich Hölderlin's *Hyperion* as an example of such a practice.

The second field, which can once again be divided in two, is concerned with the breeding and production of completely new creatures. Almost as in religious myths, creatures are created by a creator. The starting point is

---

[312] Cf. Anna Sieben, Katja Sabisch-Fechtelpeter and Jürgen Straub, "Menschen besser machen. Terminologische und theoretische Aspekte vielgestaltiger Optimierungen des Humanen", in Anna Sieben, Katja Sabisch-Fechtelpeter and Jürgen Straub (Ed.), *Menschen machen. Die hellen und dunklen Seiten humanwissenschaftlicher Optimierungsprogramme*, Bielefeld 2012, 27–79, p. 39.
[313] Ibid.
[314] Michel Foucault, *The History of Sexuality, vol. 2: The Use of Pleasure,* trans. Robert Hurley, New York 1990; Michel Foucault, *The History of Sexuality, vol. 3: The Care of the Self*, trans. Robert Hurley, New York 1988; Sloterdijk, *Du musst dein Leben ändern*, 510–520; *You must change your Life*, 442–452.

no longer man as he exists; still less is man the final product. The being that is created in these narratives is recognized by both himself and society as being in some respect deficient as compared to man as he actually exists. I will look at Goethe's Homunculus, as well as at the mechanical puppets of Kleist's "Marionettentheater" as examples of such artificial men or machines. Whereas in the first variant of anthropoetics it is the precarious existence of the human being that must be optimized and the anthropological that must be technologized, in the second variant, in which man is absent, it is rather technology that must be anthropomorphized. There are many programmatic texts on the above topic, since the history of anthropotechnics is coextensive with its being reflected in literature.[315] This investigation will in any case confine itself to technological, experimental, and optimizing experiments in German literature. Goethe's, Kleist's and Hölderlin's anthropotechnical tendencies will be considered in a manner parallel to the consideration of Campanella, Kant, Humboldt and Key on the cultural-scientific level.

1. The Technologization of the Human

1. Technologization from the Outside: Faust's Enhancement

The first anthropotechnic category describes the optimization of existing individuals. Prosthesis, as well as enhancement, can be placed under this heading. It has an external point of contact with the individual. What can already be discerned is that the relatively broad concept of prosthetics that is operative here can generally be understood in the etymological sense of a "supplement". That does not mean, however, that the distinction between enhancement and prosthetics can be entirely nullified, since in contemporary biotechnology prosthetics are overwhelmingly thought of as "healing". But to think of prostheses as purely mechanical and as an external object added to the body – like the artificial hand of Goetz von Berlichingen – seems, in the advent of tissue engineering, to be conceptually one-sided, because these technologies will allow human engineering

---

[315] From Ovid's *Pygmalion* to Shelley's *Frankenstein* to Houellebecq's *Humanum*, the thematic list of the trans- and posthuman seems almost unmanageable; cf. Horst Albert Glaser and Sabine Rossbach, *The Artificial Human*, Frankfurt a. M./Bern/New York 2011.

to directly intervene *in* the body, instead of simply modifying it from the outside.

In the following, prosthesis is characterized as a type of optimization in which man necessarily objectifies himself. The traditional, technical definition of prosthesis, which in the past designated the other, that which is foreign to the human body, is now, through new technologies, absorbed into the human body and thereby becomes part of the human organism. Prosthesis can be understood as something man makes himself, something with which he can experiment on and which he can operate. If prosthesis was traditionally something "supplementary", we can today ask whether the human has not become that which supplements modern prosthesis. This investigation works with an understanding of the "supplement" as something external that operates on a passive human being. Through prostheses, surgery, medication (doping), and also through discipline and education, human performance and vitality can be increased.

There is an increased consciousness of the body in modernity, and it is a consciousness in which, instead of the body being worked *with* as in earlier centuries, the body is increasingly worked *upon*. This work seeks to bring about the self-actualization of the body, a process that can be increased exponentially. We might think here of the artists Marina Abramović's and Ulay's remark: "aesthetics without ethics is cosmetics."[316] Man must become as beautiful, as intelligent, and as strong as he possible can; he no longer takes his natural state to be his fate. He builds his own body aesthetically, following his wishes and his imagination. The operable man demands a limitless vitality; he rebels against the process of aging, which cannot be naturally reversed, as well as against the incompleteness of his body. "The current key term for these externalized increases in outward application is 'enhancement', a word that expresses the shift of emphasis from the previous practising-ascetic self-intensification (and its bourgeois translation into 'education' (Bildung)) to the chemical, biotechnical and surgical heightening of individual performance profiles. The enhancement fever of today articulates the dream – or the illusion – of a modernization that does not stop at formerly internal zones in human self-relationships."[317]

---

[316] Abramović and Ulay, quoted from Dominic Johnson, *The Art of Living: An Oral History of Performance Art*, London 2015, 17.

[317] Sloterdijk, *Du musst dein Leben ändern*, 530; *You must change your Life*, 337.

But what does this "enhancement" mean for man and his fundamental anthropological characteristics? "In bioethics the concept of enhancement usually designates interventions that are meant to improve the human form or human performance past the point needed to maintain and reproduce health."[318] An increase "past the point" thus means that enhancement no longer just heals, but optimizes. Man, "the creature of defects" (Mängelwesen), can thus balance out his natural deficits and secure an advantage for himself by enhancing his performance – particularly in the modern culture of competition and acceleration. In the words of Jean-François Lyotard, the imperative that holds for these technologies of the self is "be operational (that is, commensurable) or disappear."[319] In this way, sex hormones and vitamins optimize the underperforming body. With the aid of these "biopolitical agents", man first becomes aware of the deficiencies of his own body and mind and second learns to increase himself and complete himself without much training or strenuous labor.[320] A connection can be drawn here to Goethe's *Faust* (1805/1832): the "Witches' Kitchen" dramatizes the optimization of age (rejuvenation) and thus can be understood as a kind of magical hormone therapy.

Through various interventions, modern man has today opened up the possibility of emancipating himself from his own body, particularly by objectivizing it. Pharmaceutical technology makes it possible to form a new man, while the material modification of our subjectivity by means of psychotropic and nootropic substance (anti-depressants, Prozac, Ritalin, etc.), as well as by genetic technologies makes a new logic and a new ontology necessary.[321] Faust famously says "Two souls dwell, alas! reside within my breast" – body and spirit.[322] He can now act on both, both serve as points of intervention. When nothing is secure or stable any longer, when not

---

[318] Eric T. Juengst, "Was bedeutet Enhancement?", in Bettina Schöne-Seifert and Davinia Talbot (Ed.), *Enhancement*, Paderborn 2009, 29–46, p. 29.

[319] Jean-François Lyotard, *The Postmodern Condition: A Report on Knowledge*, trans. Geoff Bennington and Brian Massumi, Minneapolis 1984, xxiv.

[320] Heiko Stoff, "Eine Geschichte der Dinge und eine dingliche Geschichte des Menschen. Methodische Probleme", in Vienne and Brandt (Ed.), *Wissensobjekt Mensch*, 43–67, p. 57.

[321] Cf. Nikolas Rose, *The Politics of Life Itself. Biomedicine, Power, and Subjectivity in the Twenty-First Century*, Princeton 2006; Rose, "Neurochemical Selves", *Society*, 41/November/December 2003, 46–59.

[322] We take the Hamburg edition of Goethe's works (hereinafter HA), edited by Erich Trunz, München 1982–2008, here Vol. 3 Dramatic Poems I as a basis, here Goethe, HA 3, 41, V. 1112. The edition is based on the *Faust* text in the 12th volume of the

74

only genes but also the body itself has lost its static character as an object, a multifunctional intervention into and onto the body becomes possible. Man is now able to create his own polyvalent self through these interventions as well as to deconstruct his old self in order to divide himself into multiplicities.[323] This anthropological opportunity to create is nowhere so apparent as it is in the literary figure of Faust. Faust is the prototype of the man who raises himself from being *subject* to *project*. Mephisto's magical assistance offers him the chance to become his own surgeon, meaning that "biology [...] is no longer destiny."[324] Thus Faust disdains "the toil of action," which would take the form of "sustained training." This is a training that is primarily associated with slow learning. Ironically, after Faust expresses skepticism about the witch and her potions, Mephisto offers Faust a more circuitous means of rejuvenation: "A recipe/ that takes no money, magic, or physician:/ Go out at once into the country/ and set to hoeing and to digging;/ confine yourself – and your thoughts too – / within the narrowest spheres;/ subsist on food that's plain and simple,/ live with your cattle as their peer, and don't disdain/ to fertilize in person fields that you will reap./ Take my word for it, there's no better way/ to remain young until you're eighty".[325] Faust, who wants to achieve bodily optimization with-

---

last hand edition (*Goethes Werke*, Stuttgart/Tübingen 1832, Cotta). There are only a few fragmentary manuscripts of *Faust I* (exception V. 3620–3775). *Faust I* was completed in 1806, but due to the turmoil of the war, it could only be published in 1808, as the 8th volume of Goethe's works, at Cotta. The scene "Witches' Kitchen" dates from 1788–1790 and was already sketched out during Goethe's Italian journey (1786–1788) and printed in 1790. For a detailed explanation of the text tradition see HA, vol. 3, 756–761, and Waltraud Hagen and Edith Nahler (Ed.), *Quellen und Zeugnisse zur Druckgeschichte von Goethes Werken*, vol. 1, Berlin 1966. For a detailed overview of Faust as well as Goethe's work phases, see Ulrich Gaier, *Kommentar zu Goethes Faust*, Stuttgart 2002, 307–313, on the "Hexenküche" in particular, 78–84. On the metrical design of the scene Markus Ciupke, *Des Geklimpers vielverworrner Töne Rausch*, Göttingen 1994, 60ff. English Version: Johann Wolfgang von Goethe, *Goethe's Faust: Parts I and II*, trans. Stuart Atkins, Princeton 2014, 30.

[323] The fact that not only Mephisto but also Faust is constantly changing and taking on other roles is shown on the one hand by his connection with Gretchen, but also by his appearance at the imperial court, his relationship with Helena, and his acting as a big industrialist at the end of the drama. Faust constantly redesigns himself in the drama, thereby also channeling his continuous quest.

[324] Rose, *The Politics of Life Itself*, 40.

[325] Goethe, HA 3, 76, V. 2352–2361; *Goethe's Faust*, 60. Mephisto gives similar advice in *Faust II*, Act 1, "Imperial Palatinate", to the emperor: "Take a hoe and spade, dig yourself, [...]" (ibid., 5039ff).

out expending any effort, immediately refuses this "devilish" offer: "That's work I am not used to, nor can I bear the thought/ of having to do labor with a shovel./ A life so much constricted would never do for me."[326] Faust unconditionally rejects the "traditional" work that forms the self gradually. He wants, typically for the possibility of enhancement, immediate effects. Faust turns Horace's "*carpe diem*" into: "amuse yourself". Since all theory is "gray" and, if Mephisto is to be believed, "the golden tree of life is green"[327], Faust, whose heart is "cured of the thirst for knowledge"[328], can only be refreshed by heading out "into the world".[329] The problem for Faust, who is over 50, is his age. Thus, before he does anything else, the doctor must intervene against time, as well as against his genes. He neither wants nor is able to tolerate his deficits. "Yet as you see from my long beard/ I lack all nonchalance of manner."[330] An ideal of youth, beauty, and vitality until death – a world without pain, suffering, worry, hardship, and boredom – lacks any rational basis, yet Faust, as the prototype of modern man, wants to see his longing for an "anesthetization of the finite experience" fulfilled.[331] Since, in the normal world, without supplemental means, this change is unachievable, the only means available to Faust are those that the 20th century would later take up. Man, "creatures of defects", must be healed by an external intervention. Vitaminizing (yielding a high-performing body) and harmonization (i.e., the optimization of sexual potency and age) are not only "the central biopolitical technology" of the 20th century.[332] In the literary figure of Faust, they constitute a synthesis of mastery, self-care, and knowledge. Thus, already in the first part of the drama, Faust leaves the ground of human existence, in the strict sense, behind. Once Goethe's protagonist has noticed that he cannot improve himself through self-cultivation (Bildung) and knowledge, he must improve himself through "breeding".

In *Urfaust*, Faust is still a young professor and needs no magical assistance to be rejuvenated. It is only in the final drama that Goethe allows Faust, as an old man, to walk down the path of black magic, so that he can

---

[326] Ibid.

[327] Ibid., V. 2038ff, *Goethe's Faust*, 52.

[328] Ibid., V. 1768, *Goethe's Faust*, 45.

[329] Ibid., V. 1829; *Goethe's Faust*, 47.

[330] Ibid., V. 2055ff; *Goethe's Faust*, 52.

[331] Oliver Müller, *Zwischen Mensch und Maschine. Vom Glück und Unglück des Homo faber*, Frankfurt a. M. 2010, 116.

[332] Stoff, "Eine Geschichte der Dinge", 59.

plunge into sensuality with Mephisto's aid. Faust, who is only externally, but not spiritually, passive, must grasp his body as a material, as something plastic and formable, in order to overcome his boundaries. He will no longer allow his body to dominate him and determine him: now it is he who will build his body. Faust's method is thus an existential experimentalism that aims to remove the limits of the human body.[333] Through the removal of these limitations, Faust reveals himself to be a transgressor of boundaries who, with Mephisto's assistance, experiments with various human modifications. The constant stimuli which his rejuvenation allows him to experience push him towards enhanced performance and productivity. Mephisto counts "Cupid," who "race[s] to and fro", among these stimuli. Faust, the new-born sensualist, soon sees "in every woman a Helen of Troy."[334] After his rejuvenation, two hearts really do pump in Faust's breast. The clock of his life has been turned back. Faust's "rebirth" is not portrayed as a spiritual rebirth, but rather as purely of the body.[335] Mephisto knows this new life force and spurs on the rejuvenated man: "And, now, away! You must keep moving, [...] It is essential that your body sweat."[336] The optimized body must move itself so that the magic "elixir" can be distributed through the body's circulatory system.[337] Faust, who wants to traverse not only the bodily but also the spiritual borders of his subjectivity, is not driven to religion by his transcendental "homelessness" but rather burrows himself more deeply into the earthly, the material, and the bodily. His external appearance is tuned up, his performance is enhanced, and this external appearance now catches the attention of others.[338] After his first contact with Gretchen, in the scene titled "Street", Gretchen is struck not by the freshly rejuvenated professor's "debonair" saying, but rather by his appearance, which is that of a "gentleman" and thus suggests "a noble birth".[339] Gretchen is practically applying the science of physiognomy to Faust when she says that she can read his heritage

---

[333] What fails with the earth spirit as an attempt to dissolve mental boundaries, Mephisto leads with the witch into a physical plane and is successful (cf. V. 482–520).

[334] Goethe, HA 3, V. 2598, 2604; *Goethe's Faust*, 66.

[335] Douglas F. Bub, "The Crown Incident in the Hexenküche: A Reinterpretation", *Modern Language Notes*, 3 (1958), 200–206, p. 205.

[336] Goethe, HA 3, V. 2587, 2594; *Goethe's Faust*, 66.

[337] Ibid., V. 2519, 2595ff; *Goethe's Faust*, 64, 66ff.

[338] Ibid., V. 2605-2610; *Goethe's Faust*, 69.

[339] Ibid., V. 2680ff; *Goethe's Faust*, 69ff.

"from his eyes and forehead".[340] On the one hand, the body becomes a medium of communication that is discussed by the characters; on the other hand, it makes communication possible. This point becomes even more palpable in the "Garden" scene – not only when Gretchen calls her hand "so ugly" and "rough", but also when Faust himself is inspired to mention Gretchen's appearance, even when Gretchen introduces another topic.[341] What he has to say in response to Gretchen's story about her dead little sister is almost cynical: "An angel, if like you."[342] We might say that Faust's new body can only perceive other bodies. But Gretchen too only notices the old professor because he has been rejuvenated and Faust, for his part, upon encountering the "lovely girl", feels overwhelming "desire for the sweetness of her body."[343] His designation of Gretchen as a "sweet young thing" whom he can have "lying in his arms" has clear physical connotations.[344] It is only through the complete regeneration of his youth that it is even possible for Faust to strike up conversation with Gretchen. In this sense, we can say with certainty that rejuvenation is constitutive of the cure itself. The scenes with Gretchen are, in any case, not the only ones in which it is precisely the young, active body (or flesh, in the sense of a body without a soul) that stands at the midpoint of action and communication. In an earlier scene, "Before the Gate", we see Faust on his walk as a man still sensitive to youth, the appearance of which he nonetheless experiences as contrary to his own, since he feels himself aged before his time.[345] Faust can even join in the jubilation and dance of the people and gladly returns their "thanks and wishes of good health".[346] He remains, however, a spectator on the sidelines, since his body is not compatible with their celebration. The scene in which Faust signs his pact with Mephisto more pointedly shows that Faust is torn between a young spirit and an old body: "I am too old to live for pleasure only/ too young to be without desire."[347] It is through his body that Faust feels the cleft that separates him from life's pleasures.

---

[340] Ibid., V. 2682.
[341] Ibid., V. 3082; *Goethe's Faust*, 79.
[342] Ibid., V. 3124; *Goethe's Faust*, 80.
[343] Ibid., V. 3327ff; *Goethe's Faust*, 86.
[344] Ibid., V. 2619; *Goethe's Faust*, 67.
[345] Ibid., V. 903–940; *Goethe's Faust*, 26.
[346] Ibid., V. 992; *Goethe's Faust*, 28.
[347] Ibid., V. 1546ff; *Goethe's Faust*, 40–41.

The addition of Faust's rejuvenation that takes place between the *Ur-faust* and *Faust* is thereby decisive, since it is not only the sensual capacity for connection – in the youthful sense of falling in love – that is lost, but time itself. Mephisto assures Faust that "a new career" is only possible through a new body.[348] Here we clearly see just how dependent spirit is on its material basis. Faust can only become "God's image", a "super-man [*Übermensch*]", "fearless" or "capable" when he is strong.[349] When his bodily disposition is precarious, the possibilities of his existence are rapidly diminished.

The scene in the "Witches' Kitchen" can be read as a vision of transhumanism, which, in the last analysis, consists of overcoming the deficiencies of the human body. Faust, the human being, is improved, given an abundance of life, regenerated, and so is more active than his fellow human beings. If modernity is the epoch of enhancement, then Faust is its prophet. He is one of the first modern literary characters who raises the practice of doping to a maxim: "I am too old to live for pleasure only/ too young to be without desire."[350]

In the investigation of rejuvenation, what is crucial is not the characterization of Faust as a modern individual, affirmative of and open to administering drugs, but rather the demonstration that the stylization, the aestheticization, and the experimental optimization of Faust's character occurs through technologies that mirror contemporary conceptual structures. The body here is characterized as a malleable object. For Faust wishes to intervene into his own body, his own self, into his phenotype as though into something external and other. Thus, man turns himself into an object. The care of the self is externalized as enhancement in the scene in the witches' kitchen. The subject Faust cancels the limitations of "body-time" and is thus able to exceed the limits of a classical anthropology.[351] The body is "no longer a holy and untouchable 'fate dictated by nature', but rather changeable and malleable."[352] The body becomes an instrument. Faust shows the reader the promise of a technological existentialism unfolding

---

[348] Ibid., V. 2072; *Goethe's Faust*, 52.

[349] Ibid., V. 516, 490, 439, 385; *Goethe's Faust*, 16.

[350] Ibid., V. 1546ff; *Goethe's Faust*, 40–41.

[351] Klaus Hoyer, *Exchanging human bodily material: Rethinking bodies and markets*, London 2013, 94.

[352] Kurt Bayertz and Kurt W. Schmidt, "'Es ist ziemlich teuer, authentisch zu sein…!' Von der ästhetischen Umgestaltung des menschlichen Körpers und der Integrität der menschlichen Natur", in Johann S. Ach and Arndt Pollmann (Ed.), *No Body is perfect. Bau-*

itself into a radical freedom, a radical novelty. Freedom thus becomes complete creative power over the anatomical and temporary boundaries of life. Traditional limits are destroyed by these titanic acts on Faust's part. "A curse upon the nectar of the vine!/ A curse upon love's highest favors!/ A curse on hope! a curse on faith!/ but cursed be patience most of all!" All that remains is for the chorus of spirits to express their lament, and sweep up the shards. "Grief and woe!/ A beautiful world/ that, by your violence,/ has been destroyed,/ collapses and shatters,/ crushed by a demigod!"[353] Faust, the individual, thus becomes the autonomous planner of a "new life", showing decisively that bodies are no longer born, but made.[354]

2. Working on Oneself from Inside: Hyperion's Technologies of the Self

Introspective technologies of the self are the opposite of enhancement, or a supplementation from the outside. The individual is responsible for the selection of the correct methods and technologies that are supposed, from the inside out, to give his life an optimal form and to aestheticize it. This last point is no less crucial in this context than outward beauty was in *Faust*. With the phrase "technologies of the self", I am referring to Foucault's investigations into the ethics of antiquity, but I am also taking up an aspect of Sloterdijk's philosophy. Sloterdijk often discusses his artistry of training in the same vein as Foucault.[355]

Historically speaking, there have always been technologies by means of which one has produced oneself. Two technologies were prevalent in Greek antiquity from the beginning. First, there was the injunction 'know oneself' (*gnôthi sautón*) and, second, there has been the exhortation to take care of oneself (*epmelesthai sautou*).[356] Foucault claims that "turning one's

---

maßnahmen am menschlichen Körper – Bioethische und ästhetische Aufrisse, Bielefeld 2006, 43–62, S. 59.

[353] Goethe, HA 3, V. 1603–1612; *Goethe's Faust*, 42.

[354] Ibid, V. 1622; *Goethe's Faust*, 42.

[355] This literary selection of texts is also contingent: it could have turned out differently. A self-technique of aesthetics can also be found in novels of education (Bildungsromane), in which the protagonist goes through a process of optimization or education, or in auto-biographical writings, which only conceive the subject and the author through writing.

[356] Cf. Michel Foucault, *Technologies of the Self. A Seminar with Michel Foucault*, ed. Patrick H. Hutton, Luther H. Martin and Huck Gutman, London 1988.

life into an object for a sort of knowledge, for a *techne* – for an art" was a central aspect of Greek antiquity.[357] We must note here that a praxis always accompanies these anthropotechnical technologies of the self, since there is no reflection without operation. These technologies must be "learned" practically. "No technology, no professional capability can be gained without a praxis, one cannot learn the art of life, the *techne tou biou* without an *askesis*, which must be regarded as self-instruction."[358] Thus a praxis, whose goal is an "aesthetics of existence", must be learned as well as practiced.[359] Such an aesthetic, according to the philosopher Wilhelm Schmidt, constitutes a modern "art of living for a wider goal beyond knowledge, combined with a training of the body (*askesis*), as a true 'art of life'."[360] In this sense, Schmidt speaks of a "formation of the self" and a "formation of life" in which man regards his life as an artwork. Canguilhem showed how it was not possible to have a science of the living "without taking into account, as something essential to its object, the possibility of disease, death, monstrosity, anomaly, and error."[361] In Canguilhem's language, one could say that his fundamental insight was to show that life is not about the normal or normality, but about normativity, namely the creation of new norms. "Life is the formation of forms."[362] But what exactly does the "art of life" mean? In this composite "art of life", art's significance lies not only in its *aesthesis* (perception), but also in its *techne* (production). Foucault also identifies aesthetic technologies of the self as "those intentional and voluntary actions by which men not only set themselves rules of conduct, but also seek to transform themselves, to change themselves in their singular being and to make their life into an *oeuvre* that carries certain aesthetic

---

[357] Foucault, *Power: Essential Works of Foucault, 1954–1984*, ed. James D. Faubion, New York 2000, 271.

[358] Ibid. Cf. Paul Patton, "Technology (of Discipline, Governmentality, and Ethics)", in Leonard Lawlor and John Nale (Ed.), *The Cambridge Foucault Lexicon*, New York 2014, 503–508, p. 504.

[359] Foucault, *The History of Sexuality: 2*, 89; Foucault, *The Courage of Truth. The Government of Self and Others II: Lectures at the Collège de France 1983–1984*, trans. Graham Burchell, New York 2011, 162.

[360] Wilhelm Schmid, *Philosophie der Lebenskunst*, Frankfurt a. M. 1998, 72.

[361] Foucault, *Aesthetics, Method, and Epistemology: Essential Works of Foucault, 1954–1984*, ed. James D. Faubion, New York 1998, 474.

[362] Canguilhem, *Knowledge of Life*, xix. Cf. Eduardo Mendieta, "Life", in Lawlor and Nale (Ed.), *The Cambridge Foucault Lexicon*, 254–262, p. 256.

values and meets certain stylistic criteria".[363] In Sloterdijk's view, the act of producing oneself has always contained a technical residue, as an act of artificial self-creation. Artificial has the simultaneous double meaning of *künstlich* (false) and *künstlerisch* (artistic). The *homo mirabile* of Sloterdijk is "as the appeal to the welcome confounding of art and life, and the equally welcome mingling of heroes, saints and artistes."[364] The subject gains a power over itself through this technology – it becomes its own creator. Thus "design" becomes a hermeneutics of technology, because "design forms life."[365] Here, as in Faust, leading one's own life becomes a project, albeit lead from inside rather than outside. Sloterdijk, like Foucault, is referring to the fact that the autonomous subject is the effect of a media auto-symbiosis, through which the subject experiences itself as transcendental. It creates itself and a world *for itself*. "The subject is everything that attempts to become and to be its own world."[366] It might seem, however, that with the technologies that accompany the notion of the self as a project, the more limited concept of anthropoetics is left behind. But such a technology of the self can be regarded as a kind of (autonomous) optimization from the inside out. The goal of this technology is no longer a more rational, healthier, or even more moral humanity, but rather an artistic life of one's own. A life that one can "affirm" on the basis of its "beauty". Aestheticization becomes optimization.

In the following, I will examine these aesthetic technologies of the self by looking at Friedrich Hölderlin's *Hyperion, or the Hermitage in Greece* (1791, 1799) as well as the theories of Romanticism. It can be schematically said of Romanticism that in it life undergoes aestheticization.[367] It is in this sense that Novalis speaks of an "art" of living by which he means leading one's individual life, and wherein this act of leading is aestheticized.[368] In this process, a model of the world is sought that is identi-

---

[363] Foucault, *The Use of Pleasure*, 10–11; Foucault, *Ethics, Subjectivity, and Truth: Essential Works of Foucault, 1954–1984*, ed. James D. Faubion, New York 1997, 225.

[364] Sloterdijk, *Du must dein Leben ändern*, 514–515; *You must change your life*, 328.

[365] Bolz, *Das Gestell*, 105.

[366] Sloterdijk, *Eurotaoismus. Über die Kritik der politischen Kinetik*, Frankfurt a. M. 1989, 183.

[367] Herbert Uerlings (Ed.), *Theorie der Romantik*, Stuttgart 2009, 9–43; 79–134.

[368] Novalis, *Schriften. Die Werke Friedrich von Hardenbergs*, Historisch–kritische Ausgabe, ed. Richard Samuel, Hans-Joachim Mähl and Gerhard Schulz, Stuttgart 1960ff, Vol. 2, 413. For the important connection between technology and romanticism, see Mark Co-

cal with oneself, since in the best possible case "each person can be an artist."[369]

In Hölderlin's *Hyperion* we encounter self-optimization as self-aestheticization.[370] His overwhelmingly monological epistolary novel is already distinguished by a certain stylization, because Hyperion writes his recollections to his friend Bellarmin and thus "inscribes" himself biographically, as well as aesthetically, in the act of narration. Hyperion's recollections stimulate a process of reflection in which the narrator modifies his understanding of himself through his narration. At the same time, he models his own life as a narrative, in which dissonant individual reflections are "integrated into new totality and continuity".[371] Thus Hyperion can interpret his life in retrospect "like the sound of a lyre on which the master runs through every tone, blending discord and harmony in obedience to a hidden plan."[372] Despite Hyperion's problematic path through life, which, because he moves between rapture and disappointment, cannot be read purely as *Bildung* (as we might be able to do with Humboldt, for example), it is nonetheless apparent that the protagonist is aestheticizing himself over the course of the novel, because the novel's concern is the "resolution of dissonances in a particular character".[373] The literary scholar Wolfgang Braungart accordingly calls *Hyperion* a "novel-experiment that tests the possibilities of an uncertain life project and reflects on it a literary man-

---

eckelbergh, *New Romantic Cyborgs: Romanticism, Information Technology, and the End of the Machine*, Cambridge (MA) 2017, for Novalis see 27–34.

[369] Ibid., 541, 497.

[370] We refer here to Friedrich Hölderlin, *Sämtliche Werke, Große Stuttgarter Ausgabe*, (hereinafter referred to as StA), published by Friedrich Beißner, Adolf Beck and Ute Oelmann, Stuttgart 1943–1985; as early as 1792–93 Hölderlin was already working on a Greek novel. A fragment of *Hyperion* was published in Schiller's *Thalia* in 1794, but a continuous work was not completed until 1795. The first volume was published in 1797 and the second in 1799. For the long process of creation and the individual versions, see Hölderlin, StA, Vol. 3, 295–335, and Lawrence Ryan, "Hyperion", in Johann Kreuzer (Ed.), *Hölderlin-Handbuch*, Stuttgart/Weimar 2002, 176–197, 176ff.

[371] Ryan, "Hyperion", 177.

[372] Hölderlin, StA 3, 47; *Hyperion and Selected Poems*, ed. Eric L. Santner, New York 1990, 37. Already here one recognizes that Hyperion metaphorically locates his life in art (here music).

[373] Ibid., 5; *Hyperion and Selected Poems*, 1.

ner."[374] In this novel, as *"terra incognita* within the realm of poetry," as Hölderlin called it,[375] we can discern the same destructive "hermeneutic life" identified by Braungart.[376] Hyperion's goal, as he expresses it at the end of the first book of the first volume, is only to realize the beauty of life: "Beauty is the meaning of life! It is one and all!"[377] "Perfect human nature," in the image of the Greeks, is the starting point he chooses for his striving.[378] Thus poetry and philosophy are beauty's highest representatives.

Despite his noble goals, none of the paths along which Hyperion attempts to complete and train himself come to anything. Although Diotima calls him the "teacher" of the people, Hyperion remains passive and theoretical, since he "can only give form in spirit, but [...] cannot yet lift my hand."[379] The only work that he is able to take up after his return from Germany is the very life story that he narrates in his letters to Bellarmin. Consequently, at the end of the second book of the first volume, he ends with his intention to organize "the world according to the law of beauty", an intention that immediately fails.[380]

At the end of the novel, the reflective hermit wants to integrate suffering into the essence of beauty. Hyperion thereby recognizes suffering as part of life and accepts it: "Our soul, when it puts off mortal experiences and lives only in blessed quietness – is it not like a leafless tree? like a head without hair? [...] in the end spirit reconciles us with all things."[381] That one suffers affirms suffering because it gives meaning to life. This becomes particularly clear in the case of poetry, for it is suffering that stimulates its writing. Hyperion's question to Bellarmin, "Why do I recount my grief to you, renew it, and stir up my restless youth in me again?", can be read as

---

[374] Wolfgang Braungart, "Hyperions Melancholie" (14/07/2005), in Goethezeitportal, http://www.goethezeitportal.de/db/wiss/hoelderlin/hyperion_braungart.pdf (02/01/2020), 4.
[375] Hölderlin, StA 6, 87, letter no. 60.
[376] Braungart, "Hyperions Melancholie", 5.
[377] Hölderlin, StA 3, 52.
[378] Ibid., 80; *Hyperion and Selected Poems*, 65.
[379] Ibid., 89; *Hyperion and Selected Poems*, 73. Nevertheless, Hyperion has the will to shape himself by means of practice: "I will try my breast at the joys of the past until it becomes like steel, I will practice at them until I am invincible" (Ibid., 69).
[380] Ryan, "Hyperion", 186.
[381] Hölderlin, StA 3, 103; *Hyperion and Selected Poems*, 84.

a poetic statement rather than a pathological problem.[382] Hyperion's technology of the self, as it appears in his writing, is, on the one hand, classical catharsis. On the other hand, it is a kind of literary working over of the material of life as well as a means of producing tension. It is precisely in reflecting on one's own suffering in poetry that one leaves no room "for the rest of completion."[383] It is precisely through narration that a distance and a harmony are produced that are entirely aesthetic, not ontic. That harmony must be broken down in the next chapter, in the next book, in order to give grounds for the continuation of the poetic material. This principle is clear in Hyperion's last words, which initially seem to indicate that the symphony of his life has been completed: "Like lovers' quarrels are the dissonances of the world. Reconciliation is there, even in the in the midst of strife, and all things that are parted find one another again. The arteries separate and return to the heart and all is one eternal glowing light." But the rupture comes once more: "Or so I thought. More soon."[384] This fragmentary end is a literary cliffhanger because "poetic reflection [...] can never be closed."[385] The literary scholar Ulrich Gaier recognizes that "in a previous unheard of way, the text is only the fact, the sign of an endless process determining itself over everything that exists."[386]

These biographical failures are framed by the technology of the self that is retrospective narration. This technique appears in the narrative itself as a process, because it – like life itself – must go on. "The goal is only reached when it becomes a path once more."[387] Life and literature are analogized to an extreme degree. The hermit-narrator follows Diotima's advice and becomes a poet, precisely because it is the poet who narrates his *life* for his *entire life*.[388] He is no longer the teacher of a people because he can only write about himself "and it is only *this* work that can contain his aesthetic attempts at education. And these attempts at education are primarily

---

[382] Ibid., 102; *Hyperion and Selected Poems*, 84.

[383] Ibid., 126; *Hyperion and Selected Poems*, 104.

[384] Ibid., 160; *Hyperion and Selected Poems* 133. Cf. Hölderlins letter in StA 6, 253, letter no. 147.

[385] Ryan, "Hyperion", 195.

[386] Ulrich Gaier, *Hölderlin. Eine Einführung*, Tübingen/Basel 1993, 217ff.

[387] Manfred Weinberg, "Nächstens mehr. Erinnerung und Gedächtnis in Hölderlins Hyperion", in Günter Oesterle (Ed.), *Erinnern und Vergessen in der Europäischen Romantik*, Würzburg 2001, 97–117, p. 114.

[388] Cf. Hölderlin, StA 3, 147–149.

attempts at aesthetic self-education."[389] Aesthetic optimization is located inside, within the individual.

Thus the formation of the self that fails in life succeeds in art, which in its turn narrates life and thus achieves aesthetic completion. Narrative optimization is therefore dialectically structured, because it "sublimates" itself. "Anamnesis without poetry is empty, poetry without anamnesis is blind."[390] Hölderlin's literary protagonist does not use anthropoetics as something practical that he applies to his own person or body, but rather, on a meta-level, he models himself on the discourse of literature. We might say that Hyperion is an anthropotechnician of a second order, since his chosen form (the narrative) stylizes its content (his life path).

Hyperion is the autonomous subject referred to by Foucault and Sloterdijk with their respective understandings of a technology of the self – a subject that functions in a literary manner insofar as it acts productively, as an artist does. The loss of aesthetics is thereby regained only in anthropotechnics as a technology of the self.[391] As mentioned above, the human, as it is understood by anthropotechnics, has no stable form. At the same time, it is not formless, since it can be modified from the inside out. Man is in the position of having to "dissolve in order to become something more."[392] Hyperion compensates for this paradoxical deficit with his poetic labors, in which he achieves a holistic composition of his life, and optimizes his life as a *narrated* life.

In Hölderlin's Romantic contemporary, Friedrich Schlegel, we also encounter this tendency to connect life and art. Nietzsche's later idea of a life to which one gives a "style"[393] had already manifested itself in the literary theory of Romanticism, which wanted turn "poetry into something living and companionable, and life and society into something poetic."[394] This optimization extends past a pure care of the self into an aesthetic self-formation that stands in a reciprocal relation to literature. The auto-operative thought that man can turn himself into an operator and thus ap-

---

[389] Braungart, "Hyperions Melancholie", 11.

[390] Weinberg, "Nächstens mehr. Erinnerung und Gedächtnis in Hölderlins Hyperion", 114.

[391] Cf. Hölderlin, StA 3, 52ff.

[392] Hölderlin, StA 4, 162; Holderlin, *The Death of Empedocles. A Mourning-Play*, trans. David F. Krell, New York 2008, 147.

[393] Nietzsche, KSA 3, 530.

[394] Friedrich Schlegel, *Kritische–Friedrich–Schlegel–Ausgabe*, ed. Ernst Behler, Paderborn 1958ff, Vol. 2, 182.

ply a technology to himself would seem at first glance to refer to Romantic theories and texts. At its core, however, this notion is as much about the formation of one's life in and through art. In this sense, optimization means the producing something out of one's self: it no longer refers to "a given reality" but to "the production of one's own reality".[395] Thus literary figures do not only give form to themselves, but rather the works, as prescriptive technologies, stimulate the reader into practicing a technology of the self. This must be understood in the sense of Novalis's statement that the "true reader" is at the same time "a true author" who poses "free operations to himself."[396] The reader is not only a passive recipient, but can actively reach into the fragmentary work and continue it. Aesthetic autonomy must be extended to the role of the reader. Following Foucault, we can by analogy consider a life to be a work that "carries certain aesthetic values and meets certain stylistic criteria"[397], which the subject can continue writing with the aid of a certain technology of the self. The choice of the correct outcome (tragic or happy) lies with the subject himself.[398] Nietzsche is thus correct to ask: "What then are our experiences?" And he answers, as Hyperion might, in the key of a poetic self-technology: "What then are our experiences? Much more that which we put into them than that which they already contain! Or must we go so far as to say: in themselves they contain nothing? To experience is to invent?"[399] This narrator, who breaks off the narration of his life *for now*, gestures towards this very possibility of continuity and expansion.

---

[395] Hans Blumenberg, "Wirklichkeitsbegriff und Möglichkeit des Romans" (1964), in Hans Robert Jauß (Ed.), *Nachahmung und Illusion. Poetik und Hermeneutik 1*, München 1969, 9–27, p. 10.

[396] Novalis, *Werke und Briefe*, ed. Hans-Joachim Mähl and Richard Samuel, München 1978ff, Vol. 2, 399.

[397] Foucault, *The Use of Pleasure*, 11.

[398] Through this stylizing of death, Hölderlin's Empedocles, for example, completes his own life as a work and thus makes it harmonious and "whole". Only with the appropriate conclusion to his life can the people recognize him as a "great man" (Hölderlin, StA 4, 148).

[399] Nietzsche, KSA 3, 114; *Daybreak: Thoughts on the Prejudices of Morality*, ed. Maudemarie Clark and Brian Leiter, trans. R. J. Hollingdale, New York 1997, 75. For Nietzsche's writing of the self, see Alexander Nehamas, *Nietzsche: Life as Literature*, London 1985.

It is not simply the case that "art wants life", but also that life wants art, to integrate art into itself.[400] In this sense Hölderlin's Hyperion stylizes his life by using literature to work it over and to optimize it aesthetically. Hyperion is the literary paradigm of living one's life anthropoetically.

2. The Anthropomorphizing of Technology

The 18th and 19th centuries are dominated by the discourse of materialism and the boundaries of this discourse. Man is there understood as both a mechanical puppet and as the puppet master.[401] Inspired by Descartes' description of animals as automata, the French doctor La Mettrie accordingly describes man as a machine that has been very capably arranged.[402] The famous automata of the French engineer Jacques de Vaucanson (like "The Flute Player") as well as those of the Swiss watch-making family Jacquet-Droz ("The Writer", "The Drawer", and "The Piano Player") made the well-worn idea of the technological production of human beings seems closer to realization.[403] Literature, together with the realm of scientific research, opens itself to the possibility of man-machine hybrids and artificial human beings. It is a paradoxical openness that, on the one hand, opposes the human to the artificial while, on the other, makes man artificial and therefore reproducible. A task for the extensive research into materialistic philosophy is the closer examination of literary androids and artificial human beings. It can be noted that literature does not simply mimetically copy its scientific environment, but rather thinks through its consequences, even only fictionally. The philosophical and scientific discussions of the 18th century were supplemented and expanded by literature. Literature, in its turn, offered the sciences models of reality as well as models of possibility. It tested different experimental realities, wherein man is not simply relegated to the sidelines, as seen in the previous chapter. The human offers a contrasting foil, the mechanical and the artificial can work through and

---

[400] Ibid., KSA 1, 760. Cf. Daniel Came (Ed.), *Nietzsche on Art and Life*, New York 2014, especially Adrian Del Caro, "Zarathustra vs. Faust, or Anti-Romantic Rivalry", 143–162.
[401] Cf. Carsten Zelle, "Maschinen-Metaphern in der Ästhetik des 18. Jahrhunderts (Lessing, Lenz, Schiller)", *Zeitschrift für Germanistik*, 3 (1997), 510–520.
[402] Julien Offray de La Mettrie, *Machine Man and Other Writings*, trans. and ed. Ann Thomson, New York 1996, 7.
[403] Cf. Michael Adas, *Machines as the Measure of Men*, Ithaca/London 2014, 140; Minsoo Kang, *Sublime Dreams of Living Machines*, Cambridge/London 2011, 103–184.

improve upon it. In my analysis of the literary machine and artificial human beings, I will show that this border nonetheless remains a dialectical and porous one.

Literature imagines the genesis of the artificial human being, who is superior to the old model. The possibility of such a human being in turn shows man that he is not static, not constant. Literature holds a mirror up to man in which he can see the world, without himself in it as an entity fixed for all eternity. When the Superhuman has arrived, antiquated man must leave the scene.[404] Anthropoetics is not only of significance because its mechanical constructions of more capable man, constructions that can dispense with him, move into the foreground of our analysis, but because they show that the contemporary episteme of man will one day disappear entirely.

In the progressive technophilic manifesto *Principles of Extropy* (1998) by the noted transhumanist Max More, man's discovery of his epistemic impermanence has a pathetic sound to it: "For us, humanity represents only a transition stage in the process of evolution and we welcome the application of technology in order to accelerate our passage from the human to the transhuman or posthuman condition. [. . .] We want to overcome the traditional biological, genetic, and intellectual boundaries that limit our progress."[405] This call for a transhumanism strongly recalls the transhumanist Faust, who also saw the "liquidation"[406] and, as the philosopher of cybernetics Gotthard Günther calls it, the "demythologization" of the subject as an opportunity.[407] A skepticism about the dissolution of the individual stands over against these visions of the Superhuman. This discontent about losing something "human", about not even having possessed it, is clearly present in the literary treatment of the character of Homunculus by Goethe. The artificial being, created in a test tube, regards himself and is regarded by society as something deficient. The same thing that defines

---

[404] Cf. Rüdiger Görner (Ed.), *Tales from the Laboratory. Or, Homunculus Revisited*, München 2005.

[405] Max More, "Principles of Extropy" (1998), quoted from Martin G. Weiß, "Die Auflösung der menschlichen Natur", in Weiß (Ed.), *Bios und Zoe. Die menschliche Natur im Zeitalter ihrer technischen Reproduzierbarkeit*, Frankfurt a. M. 2009, 35–54, p. 41.

[406] Weiß, "Die Auflösung der menschlichen Natur", 44.

[407] Gotthard Günther, "Maschine, Seele und Weltgeschichte" (1980), in *Beiträge zur Grundlegung einer operationsfähigen Dialektik*, Vol. 3, Hamburg 1980, 228, quoted from Erich Hörl, "Die offene Maschine. Heidegger, Günther und Simondon über die technologische Bedingung", *Modren Language Notes* 23 (2008), 632–655, p. 636.

Homunculus also stigmatizes him, namely, his lack of humanity.[408] Precisely this lack of humanity, however, is thought anew by Kleist in his "On the Marionette Theater," which imagines the production of new technological forms of humanity that have as little in common with human beings as *homo sapiens* does with the ape.

Artificial beings thus strikingly demonstrate just how precarious the conceptual scaffolding around "the human," "the spiritual," or "the bodily" really is. According to the media philosopher Erich Hörl, these "technological cultures of objects" (automata, Homunculus) minimize the sovereignty of the autonomous subject to the point of erasing it completely.[409] And yet, is not such a judgment too technophobic? Do not machines and artificial human beings offer a vantage point from which man might be grasped more fully, and, now that he has a foil against which to contrast himself, from which he might be formed more perfectly? Can we not learn from created creatures (technological artifacts) and make oneself like them? Can anthropoetics show us the way here? Perhaps what Mephisto says about the Homunculus can be read not just pessimistically, but also productively: "The fact is, we remain dependent/ on the creatures we ourselves have made."[410]

I will use two literary examples to analyze this anthropoetic thesis: first, the much discussed character of Homunculus from *Faust II*, who opens a field of inquiry on the organic–technological side; and secondly the machine as a model itself in Kleist's "On the Marionette Theater," which addresses, by contrast, the technological side alone.

1. Regress, Not Progress: Goethe's Homunculus as a Model for Man

The artificially produced being called Homunculus appears in the scene entitled "Laboratory" in the second act of *Faust II*.[411] The name indicates that he has some relation to the human, since Homunculus is the diminutive

---

[408] In Homunculus this inhumanity is attached to the body, whereas in Kleist's puppets it is attached to the 'mind'.

[409] Hörl, "Die technologische Bedingung", 12.

[410] Goethe, HA 3, 214, V. 7003ff; *Goethe's Faust*, 179.

[411] Regarding the metrical design of the scene "Laboratory", it should be noted that it was mainly written in madrigal verse, whereby Homunculus, as a "higher being", uses five-note verses, which underlines further the "seriousness of the high" and the heightened

of the Latin word *homo*. The being is thus already designated as a "little man". This only partly characterizes Goethe's Homunculus, however. Although he is a small, humanoid being, he in no sense *embodies* an actual human being. Homunculus is more an artificial being – who is not *embodied* – that was created by the "mixing many hundred substances" "at the hearth" by Faust's assistant Wagner at the beginning of the drama.[412] When his experiment succeeds, Wagner announces with a mixture of pathos and scientific detachment: "A human being's being made."[413] Mephisto, who is also present at the scene, is thus completely ensnared in the classical tradition of reproduction when he naively asks: "A human being? And what enamored pair/ have you imprisoned in your flue?"[414] Advancing at a breakneck speed, technology surpasses even the devil, who remains stuck in his own body. Goethe coined the term 'veloziferisch' for the diabolical impatience. For this, the poet combines the Latin word 'haste' (*velocitas*) with 'Lucifer'.[415]

The traditional Homunculus was introduced alchemically and mystically in the text *De generation rerum naturalium* (1572) by Paracelsus.[416] Paracelsus points out two modes of procreation: "The generation or production of all natural things is a twofold one, one that occurs without all art, by nature; the other occurs *through art*, namely through alchimiam."[417] At the time of Paracelsus, it was assumed that the male seed was needed for reproduction, while the female served only as an incubator. According to this theory, it was even possible to incarnate an artificial being, a child, which was like a natural child, only smaller. Paracelsus himself assumes that life can come into being through 'putrefaction' (decay through moisture and heat). With the help of this method even the revival of dead people

---

rapture of this being (see Markus Ciupke, *Des Geklimpers vielverworrner Töne Rausch*, 112).

[412] Goethe, HA 3, V. 6849; *Goethe's* Faust, 176, 175.

[413] Ibid., V. 6835; *Goethe's Faust*, 175.

[414] Ibid. V. 6836ff; *Goethe's Faust*, 175.

[415] See Goethe in a letter to his nephew Nicolovius in November 1825, in Goethe, *Sämtliche Werke. Letters, diaries and conversations*. Frankfurt edition. Hendrik Birus et al. (Ed.), Frankfurt a. M. 1985ff, Vol. 10, 333f.

[416] Paracelsus, "De generatione rerum naturalium", in Klaus Völker (Ed.), *Künstliche Menschen. Dichtungen und Dokumente über Golems, Homunculi, Androiden und liebende Statuen*, München 1971, 43–52.

[417] Ibid., 43 [italics by K. L.].

would be conceivable. On the basis of this theory he developed his idea of the homunculus:

> Now, however, the generation of homunculi should not be forgotten. [...] [Whether] it is also possible for nature and art that a human being could be born outside the female body and a natural mother? To this I give the answer that it is not at all contrary to art spagirica and nature, but is even possible. But how such things happen and may happen, is now his process: namely that a man's sperm is putrefied in the closed cucurbit with the highest putrefaction, ventre equino, for forty days, or until it comes to life and moves and moves, which is easy to notice. After this time it will look more or less like a human being, but transparent, without a corpus. If, after this time, it is fed wisely daily with the arcano sanguinis humani, and nourished for up to forty weeks, and kept in the same constant warmth of the ventris equini, it becomes a very lively human child, with all its limbs like another child born of a woman, but much smaller. We call it a homunculum, and it is not to be reared differently from another child, with great diligence and care, until it reaches its days and mind.[418]

In Goethe, however, the character appears to have more of a biologically optimized significance. Goethe does not follow Paracelsus in the latter's treatment of a "chemical human being" as a product of the alchemy of the late Middle Ages. Rather, he is inspired by new organic and technological research. In 1828 the chemist Friedrich Wöhler succeeded in transforming inorganic material into organic material for the first time by synthesizing urea.[419] Wöhler saw a new era of human transformations opening up with the successful result of his experiment, an era in which organic material could be produced "without kidneys or even an animal being necessary to

---

[418] Ibid., 48–49. Cf. Jürgen Barkhoff, "Perfecting Nature – Surpassing God: The Dream of Creating Artificial Humans around 1800", in Christian Emden and David R. Midgley (Ed.), *Science, Technology and German Cultural Imagination*, Bern 2005, 39–56, pp. 48–50.

[419] Cf. Vgl. Manfred Osten, *"Alles veloziferisch" oder Goethes Entdeckung der Langsamkeit*, Frankfurt a. M. 2003, 51.

the process."[420] The figure of the chemist and this artificial formation of urea out of cyanic-acidic ammonia represented for Goethe an impressive, as well as a terrifying, example of the cultivation of organic substances out of inorganic matter. It stirred him to write a modernized myth of Paracelsus' "little man". Wöhler's synthesis of urea seemed to yield proof that, with the aid of a "life force" (a *vis vitalis*), an organic connection could be synthesized in the laboratory.[421] Synthetic chemistry emerges out of alchemy. It remains to be seen whether now, as the literary scholar Manfred Osten insists, through the "shock" of this radical emancipation of man from nature, Goethe uses the figure of Homunculus to imagine "postmodern utopias of breeding".[422] In any case, it is true that Goethe rewrote the scene with Homunculus after Wöhler's experiment and emphasized the organic and reproductive significance of Paracelsus's "properly living human child".

One might correctly say that in Goethe's text the Homunculus figure represents the artificial generation of human beings, because Homunculus, as a life form, did not make an "uncaused 'leap' into existence."[423] Rather, according to the philosopher Nicole C. Karafyllis, Homunculus is a "biofact" who enters into existence not immediately, but through third parties (Wagner, Mephisto). Traditional reproduction is "devalued into mere burlesque" through Wagner's experiment, because the man who "will have higher origins in the future" no longer finds it necessary to reproduce as animals do, according to Wagner.[424] The natural scientist has torn open the secret of reproduction and taken it into his own hands. With this knowledge in hand, man has become an auto-demiurge, the object of his own modifications. The zoological breeding technologies to which anthropotechnics is prone to refer are superseded in new kind of biotechnology.

But what distinguishes Goethe's biological, technological figure? Homunculus is composed of human materials, but he is nonetheless not a

---

[420] Otto Wallach, *Briefwechsel zwischen J. Berzelius und F. Wöhler im Auftrage der Königl. Gesellschaft der Wissenschaften zu Göttingen*, Leipzig 1901, Vol. 1, 206, letter from 02/22/1828.

[421] Cf. Vgl. Johannes Uray, *Die Wöhlersche Harnstoffsynthese und das wissenschaftliche Weltbild, Analyse eines Mythos*, Graz 2009.

[422] Osten, *"Alles veloziferisch"*, 53.

[423] Nicole C. Karafyllis, "Biofakte – Grundlagen, Probleme, Perspektiven", *Erwägen Wissen Ethik* 17 (2006), 547–558, p. 557. Cf. also Michael Hauskeller, *Biotechnology and the Integrity of Life: Taking Public Fears Seriously*, New York 2016, 100.

[424] Goethe, HA 3, V. 6839; V. 6846ff.

human being, since he has come "only half complete".[425] Here lies his fundamental deficit: Homunculus is spirit, abstract activity personified.[426] As a "brain intended for great thoughts", he is lacking the material of human existence: a body.[427] To be a human being means to have a body. Without birth – and this is the understandable insight of the pre-genetic epoch – there is no body, and without fixed place no identity. To have been formed in a test tube means to have a deficient and fragile existence. In this respect, Homunculus lacks a "right to exist". What he wants is "to achieve existence properly."[428] This wish proves to be difficult, however, since Homunculus represents a biotechnological breeding that takes place outside the mother's body, a being that has been compelled to throw off the "ballast" of the bodily, and that, through its pure presence, disputes the organic boundaries that were considered hard and fast in the 18th century. Such boundaries were only considered as malleable within the temporal framework of evolution even in the 19th century. In this literary figure, the gene pool of life becomes a toolbox with which one can "tinker" for optimization.[429] In this light, the Homunculus is a being who has not gone through the process of phylogenesis; instead, he was thrown into the world in a test tube by Wagner. The focus on this figure once again poses the classic anthropological question: what distinguishes man from other beings? Is it his body or his mind? These ethical and conceptual questions are not purely rhetorical. Instead, they show the problematic opened up by modern debates in genetics.

The space in which Homunculus is presented is paradigmatic for this new view of man and human reproduction. The scene direction describes a setting filled with "cumbersome apparatus designed for various fantastic purposes."[430] The laboratory as historical semantics is – and this can only be hinted at here – an *intertopos* oscillating between pre-modern alchemy or pharmacy, and modern human genetics. The laboratory as an experimental system becomes the new place of birth, of character and the rebirth of man, as well as of knowledge. Rheinberger correctly describes this

---

[425] Ibid., V. 8248; *Goethe's Faust*, 209.

[426] Ibid., V. 6888ff.

[427] Ibid., V. 6869; *Goethe's Faust*, 176.

[428] Ibid., V. 7830, *Goethe's Faust*, 199.

[429] See also Wagner's choice of technical words for the creation of the homunculus (ibid., V. 6851–6854).

[430] Ibid.; *Goethe's Faust*, 175.

spatial-theoretical thinking when he remarks that "in the laboratory the organism itself is transformed into a *locus technicus*."[431] Homunculus is not only created in a sealed-off space in his vial; he lives in such a space too and thus stands at a distance from nature. The vial as a *heterotopos* becomes, on the one hand, a condition of the possibility of his existence; on the other hand, it is also a reminder of his artificiality. "It is a curious property of things/ that what is natural takes almost endless space,/ while what is not, requires a container."[432] Coming from the experimental space, the artificial 'human-thing' is a symbol of the modern inscription of the laboratory into the body, as well for the increasingly scientific and medical nature of birth. The practical experiments of the laboratory, as Wagner praises them here, are the opposite of nature: "What's been extolled as Nature's mystery/ can be investigated, if but Reason dare,/ and what she used to let be just organic/ we can produce by crystallizing."[433] The laboratory is not only the birthplace of Homunculus as pure spirit, but at the same time the birth of the modern sciences as such. Homunculus is, therefore, an "epistemic thing" in the truest sense of the word.[434] His biotechnological subjectivity can look forwards as well as backwards in time and thereby constitutes a transtemporal encyclopedia. The secondary literature on *Faust II* is correct to call him the "sagacity of pure culture."[435] Being a "demon", a "genius", "entelechy"[436], he can, as a scientific being, not only see farther than Faust, but even farther than the pagan devil, who

---

[431] Hans-Jörg Rheinberger and Staffan Müller-Wille, "Technische Reproduzierbarkeit organischer Natur – aus der Perspektive einer Geschichte der Molekularbiologie", in Martin G. Weiß (Ed.), *Bios und Zoe. Die menschliche Natur im Zeitalter ihrer technischen Reproduzierbarkeit*, 11–33, p. 14. For the laboratory as the basis of modern science, Bruno Latour, *We have never been modern*, trans. Catherine Porter, Cambridge (MA) 1993, 18–27; Bruno Latour and Steve Woolgar, *Laboratory Life. The Construction of Scientific Facts*, New Jersey 1986.

[432] Goethe, HA 3, V. 6882–6884; *Goethe's Faust*, 176. Cf. the frequent statements concerning the fragility of the vial (V. 6881, V. 7832, V. 8093, V. 8236, V. 8251, V. 8472).

[433] Ibid., V. 6857–6860; *Goethe's Faust*, 176. For Homunculus as symbol see Dan Latimer, "Homunculus as Symbol: Semantic and Dramatic Functions of the Figure in Goethe's Faust", *Modern Language Notes*, 89 (1974), 812–820, p. 814.

[434] Cf. Hans-Jörg Rheinberger, *Toward a history of epistemic things: Synthesizing proteins in the test tube*, Stanford 1997.

[435] Hermann August Korff, *Faustischer Glaube. Versuch über das Problem humaner Lebenshaltung*, Leipzig 1938, 679.

[436] Wilhelm Emrich, *Die Symbolik von Faust II. Sinn und Vorformen*, Berlin 1943, 257.

possess no free eye and who only feels "at home where gloom prevails."[437] What Homunculus lacks corporeally is balanced out by the breadth of his knowledge, which exceeds that of any human being.[438] He is symbolically as well as programmatically correct when he says "I'll go ahead and light the way" and uses his introspective mastery of knowledge to command.[439] This contrasts with Faust and Mephisto, who do not possess the information that he does. Faust and Mephisto must follow and they are thus practically "dependent on the creatures [they] have made."[440]

However, the holistic knowledge of a rational enlightenment ("I [...] light the way") is ultimately unhelpful to the "little man", since he desires quite impatiently to achieve the condition of being a natural being.[441] As pure entelechy in a pre-existential condition, he "suffers hunger, is full of longing with full knowledge."[442] His goal is to become a human being by means of possessing a body. The human thus is manifested not only in the body, but also through its genesis *in* the body. The word "genesis" is appropriate here, since "genesis" (Greek: γένεσις and lat. *Genesis*) combines the senses of "birth", "origin", and "coming into existence". It comprises *birth* as well as *becoming*, precisely those two things that the Homunculus lacks. "Life," concludes the biologist François Jacob, "means reproduction."[443] As Goethe shows in his Homunculus character, the application of technology to reproduction not only levels out history itself, but also histo*ries*, in the plural, in the sense of biological narratives. "The human being is 'in becoming', i.e., his only mode of being is a becoming."[444] Homunculus has not passed through these anthropological components of becoming and self-cultivation (as well as training) and he now has to repeat them, phylogenetically, as active actions. This "little man" thus possesses the

---

[437] Goethe, HA 3, V. 6923–6936; *Goethe's Faust*, 178.

[438] Homunculus looks into Faust's unconscious and decodes his dreams, revealing an extraordinarily close connection between language and technology.

[439] Ibid., V. 6987; *Goethe's Faust*, 179.

[440] Ibid., V. 7003ff; *Goethe's Faust*, 179.

[441] Ibid., V. 7832; *Goethe's Faust*, 199.

[442] Karl Kerènyi, "Das Ägäische Fest. Die Meeresgötterszene in Goethes Faust II" (1941), in Werner Keller (Ed.), *Aufsätze zu Goethes Faust II*, Darmstadt 1992, 160–189, p. 185.

[443] François Jacob, *Of Flies, Mice, and Men*, trans. Giselle Weiss, Cambridge (MA) 1998, 20.

[444] Kasper Lysemose, "The Being, the Origin and the Becoming of Man: A Presentation of Philosophical Anthropogenealogy and Some Ensuing Methodological Considerations", *Human Studies* 35 (2012), 115–130, p. 123.

human capacity for the freedom of a new beginning. It is only through this self-selected beginning that, if we follow the philosopher Hannah Arendt, one can become free. "The solution, without any reference to the past, is to understand that man is, as it were, existentially predetermined for the logically unsolvable task of setting a new beginning, inasmuch as he himself represents a beginning: Insofar as man is born into the world, appears in it as a 'new' by birth, he is endowed with the ability to begin. Because he is a new man, he can begin something new."[445] And so for Arendt the natality that Goethe's Homunculus passes through is the condition for the existential fact that human beings can begin something new. Homunculus "looks human" but is not a complete human being, because he stands outside of this complex of beginning.[446] He must thereby find his way to a new beginning by a detour and this is a beginning that he chooses himself – without having been properly born (yet).

Since the artificial being itself "craves existence", he turns to two pre-Socratic philosophers, Thales and Anaxagoras.[447] Both represent different philosophical currents. Anaxagoras begins with the assumption that fire is the fundamental force of life. Thales, by contrast, sees water as the original material. When Homunculus turns to Thales, this thinker furnishes him with the entirety of evolutionary development back to its origin: "Accede to this commendable request/ and start your life at life's beginning!/ And be prepared for rapid changes,/ for you'll evolve according to eternal norms/ changing your shape uncounted times,/ with lots of time before you must be human."[448] Wagner and his technical equipment have created a being that, if we follow the philosopher Hans Blumenberg, "skipped history".[449] Thus science has created a creature too quickly. This being must compensate for this haste organically, so long as he takes "lots of time".[450] It is only by taking his time that he can participate in the "eternal norms".[451]

---

[445] Hannah Arendt, *Über die Revolution*, München 1994, 4. Ed., 272.

[446] Goethe, HA 3, V. 8104; *Goethe's Faust*, 206.

[447] Ibid., V. 7858; *Goethe's Faust*, 200.

[448] Ibid., V. 8321–8326; *Goethe's Faust*, 211. It is characteristic of Goethe's view that Homunculus does not ask his researcher father Wagner, but asks the ancient philosopher Thales.

[449] Hans Blumenberg, "Lebenswelt und Technisierung unter Aspekten der Phänomenologie" (1963), in Blumenberg, *Wirklichkeiten, in denen wir leben*, Stuttgart 1996, 7–64, p. 34.

[450] Goethe, HA 3, V. 8326; *Goethe's Faust*, 211.

[451] Ibid., V. 8324; *Goethe's Faust*, 211.

Goethe's conception of self-cultivation, or *Bildung*, becomes clear in his Homunculus figure. Goethe's conception of nature prefers evolution to revolution, because, to Goethe, "every violent, erratic [...] thing in the soul is revolting because it does not accord with nature."[452]

Finally, to what extent can an Anthropoetics that might stimulate the reader to new ways of thinking be detected here? Homunculus is not only a new genetic production but at the same time a parting of ways with – as well an optimization of – an antiquated conception of man. Goethe himself described Homunculus to Eckermann as a "mental being" that had the advantage of "passing through the entire process of humanity without having been darkened or limited."[453] Man is thus defined by Goethe as a deficient being who vacillates between "haste" (*Übereilung*) and "omission" (*Versäumnis*).[454] Could Homunculus be the "very serious joke" to which Goethe refers and thus perhaps a new, perfect type of man?[455]

Homunculus's vial shatters on Galatea's shell-chariot and he is poured out into the sea, thus kicking off evolution once more ("Give you[rself] in marriage to the ocean"), and, at the same time, accompanying the optimization of man.[456] Only here, where Homunculus begins to become a *body* and to act with other bodies, there is "Eros", "which started everything" and connects everything.[457] Homunculus can become a better human being through this process of liquification and thus, in being created once more, strives to enhance himself. "His [Homunculus' – K.L.] realization in nature, by means of his entry into the elements, purified by magic", becomes the "starting point of a *embodiment of his possibilities.*"[458] Thus Goethe gives literary form to an in-vitro fertilization as a counter-concept to a progressive and overhasty anthropotechnics. Goethe sets a synthetic symbiosis and a Hegelian sublimation [*Aufhebung*] against an analytical vivisection, typified by the laboratory experiment.

---

[452] Johann Peter Eckermann, *Gespräche mit Goethe in den letzten Jahren seines Lebens*, Stuttgart 1998, 591, (04/27/1825).

[453] Ibid., 388, (12/16/1829).

[454] Goethe, *Werke. Berliner Ausgabe*, ed. Siegfried Seidel, Berlin 1960ff, Vol. 1, 446.

[455] Letter from Goethe to Wilhelm von Humboldt, 03/17/1832, in *Goethes Briefe, Hamburger Ausgabe*, ed. Karl Robert Mandelkow, München 1988, Vol. 4, 481.

[456] Goethe, HA 3, V. 8320; V. 8465–8486; *Goethe's Faust*, 211.

[457] Ibid., V. 8477–8479, *Goethe's Faust*, 215.

[458] Victor Lange, "Faust. Der Tragödie Zweiter Teil", in Walter Hinderer (Ed.), *Goethes Dramen. Neue Interpretationen*, Stuttgart 1980, 281–312, p. 298 [italics from K.L.].

We can understand Homunculus, with the philosopher of technology Gilbert Simondon, in terms of the evolution of technological modes of existence that strive for autonomy in their own particular way:

> This [artificial] object needed a regulative external milieu in the beginning, the laboratory, workshop, or sometimes the factory; it gradually increases its concretization, it becomes capable of doing without the artificial milieu, because its internal coherence increases, its functional systematicity closes as it organizes itself.[459]

The word *organized* can be understood quite literally with respect to Homunculus. He steps out of the laboratory into life and becomes an *organism*. In this sense, by becoming part of evolution, Homunculus completes not only a humanization process, but also an enlightened self-socialization process, because he frees himself from his isolated and heteronomous initial condition and connects himself to something like a unity or a whole.

In summary, it can be said that Homunculus represents a figure of anthropoetic optimization that is supposed to conjure up a new, perfected human being. However, the method (*techne*) applied to this biotechnological quasi-person is paradoxically a deceleration. Latimer calls this creation a "new creation myth".[460] It should be briefly noted that in the verses before 8327ff Homunculus here no longer speaks in the raised five-note madrigal verse, as in the laboratory, but now, together with Proteus (v. 8464–8479), uses iambic alternating triplets, i.e. cadence rhymes, and is thus also linguistically modified.[461]

Here anthropoetics presents a regress in the truest sense and not progress. It claims, as is typical of Goethe, to apply itself in opposition to an accelerated, modern, natural science and, almost ironically, against the man produced by science, who inwardly feels the pressure to hasten himself. The artificial human slowly takes shape in nature in order to emerge from his artificiality into life once more. That this relationship between living being and artifact is blurred in the character of Homunculus

---

[459] Gilbert Simondon, *On the Mode of Existence of Technical Objects*, trans. Cecile Malaspina and John Rogove, Washington 2017, 50. See also Yuk Hui, *On the Existence of Digital Objects*, Minneapolis 2016.

[460] Latimer, "Homunculus as Symbol", 814.

[461] Ciupke, *Des Geklimpers vielverworrner Töne Rausch*, 123.

is strikingly demonstrated by Karafyllis' idea of "biofacts".[462] This term describes semi-artificial living beings and it is conceptually defined as the running together of life (Greek: *bios*) and artifact. The biofact is precisely that *natural-artificial hybrid* that can either become or grow, according to Karafyllis, but cannot be born – a biofact must be made. This designation perfectly describes the problematic position of Homunculus.

According to Goethe, nature must be allowed its long "prelude".[463] Goethe wants to enrich the intellect, through which, according to Blumenberg, man follows only "empty intentions"[464], again with reason, which is farsightedly "fulfilled intention".[465] How can something that has 'fallen out of the world' through hybrid technologies – and this has been our question from the beginning – enter once more into a natural harmony? Homunculus, who is a symbol of precisely this transgenetic, as well as chimerical, crossing of limits, is ultimately connected once more to the circular course of life. Thus he is a figure of anthropoetic optimization not because of his progressive, accelerated, technological birth in a laboratory – and therewith the measure of a "higher" type of man – but rather because he has been naturally decelerated, because he returns to the beginning of evolution. Although this Goethean deceleration forms a model for a posthumanism, the warning of the sea god Proteus about Homunculus must be heeded: "just don't aspire to the higher classes,/ for once you have become a human being/ you've reached the end of everything."[466] Man himself is far too fixed for the god of liquidity. In the aggregate condition of posthumanity there can be no more dynamic optimization for Homunculus: embodiment means crystallization and thus petrification. Homunculus, by contrast, as a third "in-between" is not yet subject to the binary coding according to which human reason operates. The philosopher Thales notes this when he says, "he seems to be hermaphroditic."[467] Perhaps the im-

---

[462] Cf. Nicole C. Karafyllis, "Ethical and epistemological problems of hybridizing living beings: Biofacts and Body Shopping", in Wenchao Li and Hans Poser (Ed.), *Ethical Considerations on Today's Science and Technology. A German–Chinese Approach*, Münster 2008, 185–198.

[463] *Goethes Gespräche*, ed. Woldemar Freiherr von Biedermann, Leipzig 1889–1896, Vol. 2, 114.

[464] Blumenberg, "Lebenswelt und Technisierung", 35.

[465] Edmund Husserl, *Gesammelte Werke. Husserliana*, Den Haag 1950ff, Vol. 2, 62, quoted from Blumenberg, "Lebenswelt und Technisierung", 35.

[466] Goethe, HA 3, V. 8330–8332; *Goethe's Faust*, 211.

[467] Ibid., V. 8255; *Goethe's Faust*, 210.

proved "man" represents the goal of a process and a passage. The question is whether man *must* take this course.

2. Peoples and puppets: Kleist's "On the Marionette Theater"

Like Goethe, in whose *Faust* the evolutionary deceleration of the artificial Homunculus was meant to depict a path of optimization for man, Heinrich von Kleist too stresses the instructive role of the technical artifact, the machine, and the marionette. With Kleist, however, what takes place is a technologically complete objectification of the human. This objectification requires – over and above Faust's optimization and the artificial "mind-man" Homunculus – a sublimation in the Hegelian sense of the word, an *Aufhebung* of man into the unreasoning machine. This understanding of the machine might seem paradoxical at first, since the machine was and is popularly believed to have been made to take care of human tasks.[468] The anthropocentric master-slave relationship is flipped in Kleist. In his essay, the machine is no servant, but rather a mentor for mankind.[469] The "robot" is no longer the slavish "worker" who handles human work and stands before man as an object, pure and simple.[470] Friedrich Heinrich Jacobi's remarks on the machine in 1815 – summing up an entire century of discourse – perfectly demonstrate this genealogy of the machine as determined, unfree. "Until now," says Jacobi, "the noble has been set against the mechanical" and thus "not only is art distinguished from handicraft", but rather "they are completely opposed and in the following way: to the

---

[468] Cf. Hermann von Helmholtz, "Über die Wechselwirkung der Naturkräfte und die darauf bezüglichen neusten Ermittlungen der Physik" (1854), quoted from Rainer Zons, "Die Machbarkeit des Menschen", in Mirhan Dabag and Kristin Platt (Ed.), *Die Machbarkeit der Welt. Wie der Mensch sich selbst als Subjekt der Geschichte entdeckt*, München 2006, 13–28, p. 15. Here we use 'puppet/marionette' and 'machine' with the same meaning, since Kleist is concerned with the technically mindless without consciousness.

[469] Cf. Markus Krajewski, *The Server. A Media History from the Present to the Baroque*, trans. Ilinca Iurascu, New Haven/London 2018, 17–85.

[470] 'Robot' is a loan word, which had the late Middle High German forms *robāt* or *robāte*, and comes from the Slavic – probably from the old Czech *robota* (heavy, laborious work; servant work, subjugation work). Similar to the Polish *robota*. Karel Čapek then coined this term in 1920 in his play *Rossum's Universal Robots* for made, human-like artificial workers who were created to do human work.

one we attribute the ability of mind and to the other the bare physical ability; to the one freedom and self-determination; to the other slavery and foreign motive."[471] Meyer-Drawe describes this solidification of thinking in dualisms by saying that the mechanical is assigned to the dead, to slavery, to heteronomy. The organic on the other hand is assigned to the living, the creative, and the individual.[472]

I will show in the following that Kleist subverts the subject-object dichotomy with respect to the human and the mechanical and he attributes the status of optimized actor to the machine.

In his text "On the Marionette Theater," which presents a dialogue between the narrator and the dancer, Mr. C., Kleist gives complex dramatic form to the problematic of reflection and intuition, mind and matter, and, thus, man and machine.[473] The text postulates that the unity of body and mind is broken and that, through reflection, 'misfortune' has come into the world. The subject (mind) stands in opposition to the object (body).[474] The advantage here is that, in this epistemic relationship, the subject can reflect on itself and its circumstances and mold them in accordance with its wishes. The downside is that man suffers because he is no longer a unified whole. Body and mind are therefore in constant conflict, because reflection damages the "innocence" of the body's language.[475] The psychoanalyst Heinz Kohut writes that in his essay, "On the Marionette Theater", Kleist deals with the problem of the "shattered (or the deeply sick) self".[476] Man accordingly oscillates continuously between divinity and animality, leav-

---

[471] Friedrich Heinrich Jacobi, "Etwas, das Lessing gesagt hat. ein Commentar zu den Reisen der Päpste", in Jacobi, *Werke*, Leipzig 1815, Vol. 2, 325–389, p. 356, quoted in Monika Schmitz-Emans, "Der Maschinenmensch als Spiegelbild der Menschenmaschine. Zur Verwertung des Automatenmotivs durch Jean Paul", in Horst Albert Glaser and Wolfgang Kaempfer (Ed.), *Maschinenmenschen. Referate der Triestiner Tagung*, Frankfurt a. M./Bern/New York/Paris 1988, 97–123, p. 99.
[472] Käte Meyer-Drawe, "Maschine", in Christoph Wulf (Ed.), *Vom Menschen. Handbuch Historische Anthropologie*, Weinheim/Basel 1997, 726–738, p. 731.
[473] Heinrich von Kleist, *Sämtliche Werke und Briefe, Brandenburger Ausgabe* (hereafter BKA), ed. Roland Reuß, Peter Staengle and Ingeborg Harms, Basel/Frankfurt a. M. 1988ff, Vol. II/7, Berliner Abendblätter I, 317–319, 321–323, 325–327, 328–329; "On the Marionette Theatre", trans. Thomas G. Neumiller, in *The Drama Review: TDR*, Vol. 16, No. 3, The "Puppet" Issue (September 1972), 22–26.
[474] Kleist, BKA II/7, 322; "On the Marionette Theatre", 24.
[475] Alexander Kosenina, "Anthropologie", in Ingo Breuer (Ed.), *Kleist-Handbuch*, Stuttgart/Weimar 2009, 243–246, p. 245.
[476] Heinz Kohut, *Die Heilung des Selbst*, Frankfurt a. M. 1981, 282.

ing no possibility of identity or fixity in his being. This instability becomes clear in the example, offered by the narrator, of the young man who unconsciously depicts the posture of the boy who pulled the thorn from the lion's paw, but as soon as he tries to repeat this, consciously and reflectively, just seems comical and loses his grace.[477] This loss is the substance of Kleist's work – because whoever forfeits "grace" has "alienated himself from the order" as well as from "the center of gravity of his being."[478] This loss is thus symptomatic of contradiction and of brokenness. The second example, which is offered by the narrator's interlocutor, Mr. C., is that of a bear, i.e., a mode of life that lacks consciousness. The bear reacts instinctively to the blows of its opponent in a fight and it therefore cannot be taken in by his feints. Mr. C. says: "Eye to Eye, as if he could see into my very soul, he stood there, his paw raised ready for combat, and whenever my thrusts were not intended as strikes, he simply did not move."[479] The philosophical anthropologist Helmut Plessner correctly designates this point in Kleist's texts as showing the "eccentric position" or eccentricity of man: "Man stands between nature and God, between that which has no self and that which is itself and nothing else. He presents his self to himself. He possesses neither the flawless precision of the marionette, nor the surety of instinct of the animal, nor the perfect originality of unerring self-actualization."[480] Already in the previous philosophical and literary examples we have seen that man has a strange disproportion to his physical existence. In the animal, as a pure body, there is no break. But in man there is a break. The break that places him between the puppet and the completed unity. So this *broken unity* is now, so to speak, the specific position of man. According to Plessner, it is precisely this broken unity that constitutes being human.[481]

In Kleist's text the first example shows that man's capacity to reflect on himself stands opposed to grace, because man can only be beautiful as a lifeless or spiritless statue. The second example, by contrast, con-

---

[477] Kleist, BKA II/7, 326; "On the Marionette Theatre", 26.

[478] Josef Kunz, "Kleists Gespräch Über das Marionettentheater", in Walter Müller-Seidel (Ed.), *Kleists Aufsatz über das Marionettentheater. Studien und Interpretationen*, Berlin 1967, 76–88, p. 80.

[479] Kleist, BKA II/7, 330; "On the Marionette Theatre", 26.

[480] Helmut Plessner, "Zur Anthropologie des Schauspielers" (1948), in Plessner, *Ausdruck und menschliche Natur*, Frankfurt a. M. 2003, 399–418, pp. 416–417.

[481] Plessner, *Philosophische Anthropologie*, ed. Julia Gruevska, Hans-Ulrich Lessing and Kevin Liggieri, Berlin 2019, 218.

trasts man and the instinct-ruled animal. These examples are framed in the text by a conversation about the dancing puppets in the marionette theater. Here Kleist offers a counter-model to human reason and contrasts it with the non-reflective material world. The "mechanics of these figures", whose "center of gravity" grants them perfect balance, displays, according to Kleist, "much grace as they dance."[482] Their pendulum-limbs react of "their own" volition in a mechanical way and are thus *autopoetically* perfected.[483] Man, as the active party, is excluded from the technological circle. No puppet master is needed to project himself into the dance of the puppet because the momentum from the electric crank is sufficient to make the spiritless puppet move. According to Kleist, the mechanical dance is so beautiful and graceful because the last bit of spirit has been removed from the puppet and its dance plays out entirely in the realm of mechanical forces.[484] The spiritless-technical thus has the advantage over the human in art forms like dance, because "the spirit cannot err where it does not exist."[485] In Kleist's text, prosthetic hybridization is discussed as a process of perfection for human beings who have mechanically optimized themselves, like, for example, the man who had a "mechanical leg" made by an "English craftsman" and can now dance "with a composure, lightness, and grace that would amaze any sensitive observer."[486] Unlike man, the machine possesses "symmetry, mobility, lightness; only all of that to a higher degree" in itself.[487] What throws human beings out of balance is their capacity to reflect. Man lacks a "natural disposition of the centers of gravity", unlike the machine.[488] In his essays *Von der Überlegung*, "On Thought", and *Über die Allmähliche Verfertigung der Gedanken beim Reden*, "On the Gradual Formation of Thoughts in Speech", Kleist privileges action over reflection. Reflections "hinder" and "oppress" the soul and bring it into disorder.[489] Kleist uses the term "affectation" here: "[...] affectation appears when the soul (*vis motrix*) locates itself at any point other than the

---

[482] Kleist, BKA II/7, S. 317; "On the Marionette Theatre", 22, 23.
[483] Ibid., 318; "On the Marionette Theatre", 22.
[484] Ibid., 319; "On the Marionette Theatre", 22.
[485] Ibid., 323; "On the Marionette Theatre", 24.
[486] Ibid., 321; "On the Marionette Theatre", 23.
[487] Ibid., 322; "On the Marionette Theatre", 24.
[488] Ibid.; "On the Marionette Theatre", 24.
[489] Kleist, "Von der Überlegung", in BKA, Vol. II/7, 301–302, p. 301; "Über die allmählige Verfertigung der Gedanken beim Reden", in BKA, Vol. II/9, 25–35.

center of gravity of the movement."[490] In contrast to the machine, man is not perfectly balanced, nor does he follow "the simple law of gravity."[491] A further advantage of the mechanical is that the puppet defies gravity – because of its strings it is not burdened by gravity, and, crucially for Kleist, it does not need to rest, to regain its strength after dancing.[492] This criterion of rest appears to be an important distinction insofar as the respective performance capabilities of machines and human beings are concerned.

What Kleist observes in puppets, Hegel sees in the lack of reflection that characterizes the heroes of antiquity. For Hegel, the ancient hero is a "total person". The strength of these great figures lies precisely in the fact that, according to Hegel, "they do not choose, but rather from birth are through and through that which they want and they carry out. They are what they are and they are that thing eternally, and that is their greatness."[493] In them, praxis does not run through theory and the deed is not interrupted by reflection. Kleist locates this humanistic model of the naïve character in the machine.

When reflection becomes "darker and weaker", then beauty – what Kleist calls "grace" – "emerges all the more shining and triumphant."[494] Hence the purest-seeming being is the one who has "no consciousness at all – or has infinite consciousness."[495] The grace of the marionettes is without inner substance and is thus "a pure aesthetics of effects."[496] But it is precisely for this reason that Kleist sanctifies the machine. The machine is more divine than man. As a result, it would be "almost impossible for a man to attain even an approximation of a mechanical being. In such a realm only a God could measure up to this matter [...]."[497] Kleist's materialistic observations can be considered technophilic, since "the articulated

[490] Ibid., BKA II/7, 322; "On the Marionette Theatre", 24.

[491] Ibid.; "On the Marionette Theatre", 24.

[492] Ibid., 323; "On the Marionette Theatre", 24.

[493] Georg Wilhelm Friedrich Hegel, *Vorlesungen über die Ästhetik III, Theorie–Werk–Ausgabe*, Vol. 15, Frankfurt a. M. 1970, 546.

[494] Kleist, BKA II/7, 330; "On the Marionette Theatre", 26.

[495] Ibid., 331; "On the Marionette Theatre", 26.

[496] Günter Blamberger, "Von der Faszination riskanter Bewegungen. Anmerkungen zu Kleists Sportbetrachtungen", in *Kleist–Jahrbuch 2007*, 38–45, p. 39.

[497] Kleist, BKA II/7, 325; "On the Marionette Theatre", 24.

puppet" is raised to the status of a reproduction of God on earth.[498] This is a conception of grace in which concept of the body and grace can be called transhumanist.

Kleist's literary treatment poses a central question that had already been thematized in the discourse of his time. But, at the same time, he inverts this discourse and pushes it to its extreme. In his view, machines are that which man has always wanted to be, but could never attain. They are his desired goal not only in the progress of their development or their speed, but, ironically enough, in their "lack of spirit". The extinguishing of the quality that raises man over all other objects becomes the final criterion for his optimization. According to Kleist, man must change programs. He can no longer attempt to be like God, but he must now perfect himself technologically.[499] The point at which this reversal takes place consequently lies at the juncture between human and inhuman forces, which latter are no longer, in a secular age, divine, but rather technological.

It did not seem possible that machines could develop the capacity for thought in Kleist's time. No machine then could be said to possess self-interest, self-perception, communication, unconscious automization, and feeling. By its very possibility, the machine, the automaton, poses a question about life (that which has a mind) and its limits. What, in classical as well as modern debates, is usually seen as a drawback in machines, namely, their mindlessness, is seen as an advantage by Kleist. In "On the Marionette Theater" he shows "how consciousness creates disorder in the natural harmony of men."[500] Machines' unreflective and emotionless bearing renders them superior to man in the surety of their charm, grace, ease, and calm.[501] The prosthetic leg is not an "affectation": not only does it function properly, it functions even better than an actual human leg. It never falls asleep, never gets tired. Machines lack the deficiency of reflective self-consciousness and for Kleist this opens up an anthropoetic space of possibility.

---

[498] Cf. Gerhard Oberlin, "Gott und Gliedermann. Das 'unendliche Objekt' in Heinrich von Kleists Erzählung 'Über das Marionettentheater'" (1810), in *Kleist–Jahrbuch 2007*, 272–288, p. 274.

[499] For a cybernetic-experimental view of the movements see Stefan Rieger, "Choreographie und Regelung. Bewegungsfiguren nach Kleist Marionettentheater", in *Kleist–Jahrbuch 2007*, 162–182.

[500] Kleist, BKA II/7, 325; "On the Marionette Theatre", 24.

[501] Ibid., 325, 322; "On the Marionette Theatre", 26.

Machines' lack of identity is, in Kleist's view, another opportunity. Their lack of reflection not only lets them dance perfectly, but also fence perfectly – machines have perfected the culture of the body in general. And so in the "Marionette Theater" the possibility of the aesthetic normalization of the body in dance is treated as a perfect expression of "the mastery of the soul."[502] This normalization is no longer applied by an educator, however, but rather by a machine, which shows the body how to move. The body's ideal type can therefore be calculated according to geometrical laws and it can be optimized accordingly. Mind itself must be materialized for a mathematization of the body to take place. The living body (*Leib*) is negated and replaced with a technologically perfected body. The subject must become an object. What Kleist heralds is the collective "restructuring" of the body "in favor the normalized capability and efficient use of the able body."[503] The body that is imagined does not need to rest or catch its breath, since it defies gravity and is capable of high aesthetic achievement. Kleist argues in the same vein as Vaucanson, the automaton designer and builder, who saw machines, with their inexhaustible stamina, as overtaking the human: "This automaton is more than a match for all of our pipers, who blow into the instrument, but cannot move their tongue with the requisite speed. Unlike them, my piper can blow whole arias with every movement of its tongue."[504] Following the maxims of Kleist's text, a perfect body capable of these features must be a technical one without consciousness. Mindlessness is thought by Kleist as optimal. Man is to realize himself most fully where he is no longer man. "Guiding marionette" becomes "guiding people."[505]

Homunculus, like Frankenstein's monster and Pinocchio, wanted to be a human being. Kleist's marionettes, on the other hand, attempt to make the reader more like a machine: *homo machinarius*.

---

[502] Andrea Grimm, "Die Rede über den Körper. Zum Körperdiskurs in Kleists Texten 'Die Marquise von O....' und 'Über das Marionettentheater'", in Heinz Ludwig Arnold, Roland Reuss and Peter Staengle (Ed.), *Text und Kritik. Sonderband Heinrich von Kleist*, München 1993, 170–176, p. 170.

[503] Ibid., 172.

[504] Jacques de Vaucanson, *Beschreibung eines mechanischen Kunst-Stucks, und Automatischen Flöten-Spielers, so denen Herren von der Königlichen Academie der Wissenschaften zu Paris durch den Herrn Vaucanson Erfinder dieser Maschine überreicht worden*, Augsburg 1748, 23.

[505] Tim Müller, *Der souveräne Mensch. Die Anthropologie Heinrich von Kleists*, Göttingen 2011, 208.

Hans Blumenberg's question about where the 'problem of technology' ultimately lies is taken up by literature, but it does not receive a univocal answer.[506] Goethe views artificial human beings and automata critically. Kleist, by contrast, sees the mechanical as a technological opportunity for divinity. What literature sees as a production of scientific knowledge depicted aesthetically consists, in fact, of multiple discourses of problematization that are of ever-increasing concern today, when technologization and prosthetics are familiar aspects of our daily life. In this way, anthropoetics can offer diagnoses and prognoses, since it is literature that can conceive of its time in terms more fluid and more dynamic than those of philosophy and the natural sciences.

---

[506] Blumenberg, "Lebenswelt und Technisierung unter Aspekten der Phänomenologie", 10.

IV. Doomed to Self-formation

"The human being can only become human through education. He is nothing except what education makes of him."[507] This quotation on learning and education has, as we have seen, the status of a pillar of Western cultural history. In most philosophies and theories, the question of learning is mostly directed to the human being, because it is considered, that "learning is a basic biological capacity which is far more developed in humans than in any other living being."[508] As creations who are "doomed to be learners", humans learn throughout their lives.[509]

Learning thus is considered to be founded in *anthropology*, but also in the means of *technological* practice (the question of *what* and the question of *how*): in addition to the classical anthropological differences between animals and humans, or humans and machines, the concept of 'learning' already refers to knowledge and (experiential) practice through its historical coinage.[510]

One might think that the term 'learning' is used purely descriptively in an inconspicuous and harmless way (to talk about the process of getting to know things and committing them to memory), but on a closer look, 'learning' appears to be far more ideologically charged. 'Learning' connects man, animal, and machine under the maxim of optimization. 'Learning' is used when people are to become autonomous, self-thinking, and responsible subjects. 'Learning' is used to describe a hierarchy of knowledge and power between teacher and student. But 'learning' also clearly refers to material processes. Not only the mind but also the body 'learns'. To sum up: through learning, man transforms himself to another (a knowing, ca-

---

[507] Kant, AA 9: 443.

[508] Knud Illeris, "An Overview of the History of Learning Theory", *European Journal of Education*, 53 (2018), 86–101, p. 86.

[509] Ibid.

[510] Cf. James Bowen, *A History of Western Education*, London 2003; Peter Jarvis and Mary Watts (Ed.), *The Routledge International Handbook of Learning*, London 2012.

pable, optimized) new subject.[511] However, learning is thus more than just a philosophical program: it is, as Agamben might say, a "dispositif" that converges to Foucault's concept of the "government of men".[512] A dispositif is "a heterogeneous set that includes virtually anything, linguistic and non-linguistic, under the same heading: discourses, institutions, buildings, laws, police measures, philosophical propositions, and so on."[513] In this sense learning can be seen as "the network that is established between these elements."[514] If we look at the concept of Machine Learning, we see that the connection between 'learning/education' and optimization is still present nowadays, in the so-called digital world. Most discussions about learning are bundled into a certain mode of anthropological argument and practice. It concerns how we deal with animals, machines, and human individuals. Learning is thus a dispositif that processes human self-relations of analogy and difference to other modes of existence.

In this book we have differentiated between two powerful concepts in the network of learning, breeding, and optimization: first, an anthropocentric, humanistic, and holistic concept. On the one hand there is a concept of optimization, that is tied to parameters such as anthropocentrism, humanism, and holism (Kant, Humboldt, Goethe, Hölderlin). This concept depends on a definition of life as wholeness, as experience, and as the "lived body" (*Leib*).[515] This kind of holistic-phenomenological concept of learning, nowadays also termed "tacit knowledge", separates man from animals and machines.[516] In this anthropocentric approach, man is viewed as the master of the animal and the machine, and the machines, but also the animals, are just servants and slaves to him. From anthropological standpoints in the battlefield between mind and material, mind always dominates over material: subject domesticates object.

---

[511] Cf. Andrea R. English, *Discontinuity in Learning: Dewey, Herbart and Education as Transformation*, Cambridge 2013.

[512] Foucault, "Power/Knowledge", 194–196.

[513] Giorgio Agamben, *What is an Apparatus?: And Other Essays*, trans. David Kishik and Stefan Pedatella, Stanford 2009, 2–3.

[514] Ibid., 3.

[515] Käte Meyer-Drawe, "Education", in Lester Embree et al. (Ed.), *Encyclopedia of Phenomenology*, Dordrecht 1997, 157–162; Anja Kraus, "Gender, the postmodern paradigm shift and Pedagogical Anthropology", in Carol A. Taylor et al. (Ed.), *Gender in Learning and Teaching: Feminist Dialogues Across International Boundaries*, Abingdon 2019, 54–67.

[516] Cf. Bosse Bergstedt et al. (Ed.), *Tacit Dimensions of Pedagogy*, Münster 2012.

On the other hand, there is the complete opposite to this anthropocentric concept of optimization: the mechanistic one. This concept can be figuratively seen in a lot of cases, such as animal breeding, physical conditioning, or, radically, in eugenics (Campanella, Key, Kleist). It is strictly bound to the parameters of body and experiment, and is conducted, for example, by dressage, training, and domestication. It is a concept of learning/optimization which denies the dominance of mind over material and, with this, an exceptional position for man in the natural world. Humans are put on the same level as animals and machines, and are thus understood as automata, stimulus-reaction models, control loops, or computers.

However, as we have shown, both concepts of 'learning' cannot be clearly separated from one another.

In these heterogeneous concepts of optimization, humans and animals are separated and connected. "The animal becomes everything it meant to be – man becomes nothing except what he learns, loves, and does."[517] In the early 20th century, when Ellen Key was able to speak openly and unashamedly of "categorical imperatives of the nerves and the blood"[518], the poet Christian Morgenstern was able to recognize these finer – and perhaps also the truer – idiosyncrasies of modern pedagogical anthropotechnics: "The main feature of all pedagogy is to be carried out unnoticed."[519] In this sense, the kernel of anthropotechnics is a conception of man in which man can degenerate into animal, or become divine.[520] Man as a pet is thus both a warning and a promise. It is the hope of going beyond the animal, and yet its project is to optimize the human being by breeding in a similar way to the animal. But, for humans to be modeled, they must not have a static form. Ever since Pica della Mirandola defined "man" in 1496 as a being whose essence is not fixed in advance, every humanism has in fact been a transhumanism: "He who asks what man is asks at the same time what he *isn't*."[521]

---

[517] Johann Heinrich Pestalozzi, "Der natürliche Schulmeister", in *Sämtliche Werke*, Leipzig 1901, Vol. 9, 349–536, p. 475.

[518] Key, *The Century of the Child*, 57.

[519] Christian Morgenstern, *Stufen. Eine Entwickelung in Aphorismen und Tagebuch–Notizen*, München 1922, 174.

[520] Giovanni Pico della Mirandola, *Über die Würde des Menschen* (1496), Hamburg 1990, 5ff.

[521] Justin Stagl and Wolfgang Reinhard, "Einleitung", in Justin Stagl and Wolfgang Reinhard (Ed.), *Grenzen des Menschseins – Probleme einer Definition des Menschlichen*, Wien/Köln/Weimar 2005, 9–33, p. 9.

Technologies only intensify the transhumanist tendencies in the modern age because technological possibilities almost entirely subvert the human.[522] The unsettling possibilities of the manipulation of biotechnology not only dissolve the traditional subject but also deconstruct significant distinctions and boundaries. The defining oppositions that have founded the Western order of knowledge and the world since the Enlightenment have been increasingly circumvented. Hence, technology breaks down the dichotomies of nature and culture, organism and machine, man and animal, and even man and woman. These carefully constructed differences are subverted and thus become porous. We have repeatedly seen that this subversion is a matter of reconfiguring and reflecting on what it means to call a certain entity 'man'. The literary as well as the historical examples provided above show just how much 'man' is his own designer, artist, and planner. Here a pragmatic view of anthropotechnics emerges, one in which "our good lies not in knowing, but in making."[523] In anthropotechnics and anthropoetics, man thus turns himself into an experiment. Nietzsche noted that "*hubris* characterizes our attitude towards *ourselves*, – for we experiment on ourselves in a way we would never allow on animals [...]."[524] The program of domestication and breeding is applied by man to himself through emerging biotechnologies as well as through machines. As we saw in Goethe's Homunculus and Kleist's marionettes, organic limits are increasingly contested. The gene pool brought about by evolution is being transformed into a universal toolbox that can be used transgenetically. "What happens is that traditional self-understandings are overcome. The dualism of subject and object is no longer operative. Information that is neither one nor the other, but occupies a third position, teaching man that he has failed to recognize himself."[525]

In this optimization discourse, the literature of anthropoetics offers the experimental possibility of showing, by mechanical as well as by organic

---

[522] Cf. Francis Fukuyama, *Our Posthuman Future: Consequences of the Biotechnology Revolution*, New York 2002; Katherine Hayles, *How We Became Posthuman: Virtual Bodies in Cybernetics, Literature, and Informatics*, Chicago 1999; Harold W. Baillie and Timothy K. Casey (Ed.), *Is Human Nature Obsolete? Genetics, Bioengineering, and the Future of the Human Condition*, Cambridge 2004; and Hans Moravec, *Robot: Mere Machine to Transcendent Mind*, Oxford 2000.

[523] Bolz, *Das Gestell*, 101.

[524] Nietzsche, KSA 5, 357; *On the Genealogy of Morality*, trans. Carol Diethe, New York 2006, 82.

[525] Meyer-Drawe, "Maschine", 733.

chimeras, just how abstract and artificial these assumed distinctions are. Alongside a hard deconstruction of the sciences, the cultural narrative of optimization in literature offers a conceptual and ontological subversion, whose reception can stimulate its readers to think further as well as to reflect critically on traditional concepts such as 'man', 'gender', 'life'. The fragile conditions of the human individual's identity are thus revealed. This discursive relationship can only be described in relations, as the scholar of communication, Vilem Flusser, points out: "we have to work out an anthropology that regards man as a knot, the point at which several fields traverse each other."[526] This knot should not only be seen in terms of neurological data, but also epistemologically. Man stands between anthropological, human-scientific, biotechnological, and informational networks of knowledge that condition one another, constitute one another, provoke one another, and subvert one another.

Given what has been said, we must apply this conceptual genealogy to anthropotechnics itself, in order to discern its programmatic intentions and to get a better sense of how it grounds itself, as well as how interdisciplinary networks are constructed from it. Following Georges Canguilhem's philosophy of science, we must not only unearth the polyvalent concepts of anthropotechnics and anthropoetics and regard them diachronically – a task whose difficulty is not to be underestimated – but we must also delimit these concepts and fill them out semantically and genealogically. "The meaning of a scientific concept is not limited to its horizontal use, with a view to other words and texts", as Henning Schmidgen says of Canguilhem.[527] "It is only by returning to the forces that have seized on a 'matter' in the present or the past can we grasp it."[528] But this archaeological work is just the beginning of our task. The above investigation can only be regarded as a first step towards the laying of this historical groundwork.

If we nonetheless take a retrospective glance at what we have elaborated in the above analysis, the task can be divided into a cultural-scientific anthropotechnics and an anthropoetics. The first part, which examined anthropotechnics, is more closely related to the realm of cultural history

---

[526] Vilém Flusser, "Gedächtnisse", in Ars electronica (Ed.), *Philosophien der neuen Technologie*, Berlin 1989, 41–55, p. 52.

[527] Henning Schmidgen, "Fehlformen des Wissens", in Georges Canguilhem, *Die Herausbildung des Reflexbegriffes im 17. und 18. Jahrhundert*, trans. Henning Schmidgen, München 2008, VII–LVIII, p. IX.

[528] Ibid.

(breeding, taming, and education, with birth politics, pedagogy/education, and eugenics as examples) with the goal of delivering a framework for the term 'anthropotechnics' as a *dispositif* of optimization. The second part, on anthropoetics, is, by contrast, systematic, since it deals overwhelmingly with autonomous and heteronomous poetic practices (enhancement, technologies of the self, biotechnologies, and the man-machine) in excerpts from various literary texts.

The above work is thus not able to cover all aspects of the almost unsurveyable fields of anthropotechnics and anthropoetics. However, in the examples examined, this little book has hopefully shown that anthropotechnics is not a mere "scandalous" concept that describes a marginal phenomenon. Everything that affects man in order to optimize him is to some degree an anthropotechnics. It is everything that one does to form man from the cradle to the grave, to guide him, to code him, to train him, to treat him therapeutically – from drilling to education. In anthropotechnics, the Kantian question "What is man?" becomes the Nietzschean question of what man can become.[529]

A knowledge of man was needed in order to make an 'ought' of an 'is'. Consequently, the "primacy of anthropology" is a "condition for anthropogenesis".[530] Anthropotechnics, or whatever one chooses to call human optimization, is therefore not an extreme phenomenon with respect to our daily lives and history, it is rather at the center of these. It is constitutive of man.

---

[529] Kant, AA IX, 25; *Lectures on Logic*, trans. and ed. Michael Young, New York 2004, 538; Nietzsche, KSA 4, 14.
[530] Canguilhem, *Knowledge of Life*, 19.

Acknowledgments

My first thanks go to the help with the translation of this book given by Michael Lipkin and Aengus Daly. I would also like to thank Niklas Straetker for the accurate and important reading of the Kant chapter and many productive conversations. I would also like to thank the series editors (Prof. Dr. Andrea Marlen Esser, Prof. Dr. Armin Grunwald, Prof. Dr. Mathias Gutmann) for including my book in this renowned series. The last, and probably most important, thanks go to Julia Gruevska, who inspired me largely.

Bibliography

Primary Sources

Anthropotechnics:

CAMPANELLA, Tommaso: »Sonnenstaat«. In: Klaus J. Heinisch (Ed.): *Der utopische Staat*: *Morus, Utopia/Campanella, Sonnenstaat/Bacon, Neu-Atlantis*. Hamburg 1993. 100–150.

CAMPANELLA, Tommaso: »City of the Sun«. In: Henry Morley (Ed.): *Ideal Commonwealths; Plutarch's Lycurgus, More's Utopia, Bacon's New Atlantis, Campanella's City of the Sun*. London 1890.

KANT, Immanuel: »Über Pädagogik«. In: Kant: *Werke in zehn Bänden*. Vol. 10. *Schriften zur Anthropologie, Geschichtsphilosophie, Politik und Pädagogik*. Ed. Wilhelm Weischedel. Darmstadt 1982. 697–776.

- *Gesammelte Werke*. Akademieausgabe. Ed. Preussische Akademie der Wissenschaften. Berlin 1900ff.

- »Beantwortung der Frage: Was ist Aufklärung?«. In: Kant: *Werke*. Vol. 9. Ed. Wilhelm Weischedel. Darmstadt 1983. 53–59.

- »An Answer to the Question: What is Enlightenment?«. In: Kant: *Practical Philosophy*. Trans. and ed. Mary J. Gregor. New York 2006.

- *Anthropology from a Pragmatic Point of View*. Trans. and ed. Robert B. Louden. New York 2010.

- *Lectures on Logic*. Trans. and ed. Michael Young. New York 2004.

VON HUMBOLDT, Wilhelm: »Theorie der Bildung. Bruchstück«. In: Humboldt: *Werke*. Vol. 1. Ed. Andreas Flitner & Klaus Giel. Darmstadt 2002. 234–240.

- *Werke in fünf Bänden*. Ed. Andreas Flitner & Klaus Giel. Darmstadt 1961–1980.

- »Über den Geschlechterunterschied und dessen Einfluss auf die organische Natur«. In: Humboldt: *Werke*. Vol. 1. Ed. Andreas Flitner & Klaus Giel. Darmstadt 2002. 268–295.

- »Der Litauische und der Königsberger Schulplan«. In: Lothar Schweim (Ed.): *Schulreform in Preußen 1809-1819*. Weinheim 1966. 12–15.

- *Wilhelm v. Humboldt im Verkehr mit seinen Freunden*. Ed. Theodor Knappstein. Berlin 1917.

Key, Ellen: *The Century of the Child.* trans. Marie Franzos. New York/London 1909.
Pestalozzi, Johann Heinrich: »Der natürliche Schulmeister«. In: *Sämtliche Werke*. Leipzig 1901. 349–536.
Sloterdijk, Peter: *Regeln für den Menschenpark. Ein Antwortschreiben zu Heideggers Brief über den Humanismus.* Frankfurt a. M. 1999.

- *You must change your life*. Trans. Wieland Hoban. New York 2013.

- *Du musst dein Leben ändern*. Frankfurt a. M. 2009.

- »Rules for the Human Zoo: a response to the Letter on Humanism.« In: *Environment and Planning D: Society and Space*, 27/2009. 12–28.

- *Weltfremdheit*. Frankfurt a. M. 1993.

- *Eurotaoismus. Über die Kritik der politischen Kinetik.* Frankfurt a. M. 1989.

Sulzer, Johann Georg: *Versuch von der Erziehung und Unterweisung der Kinder.* Zürich 1748.

Anthropoetics:
Goethe, Johann Wolfgang: *Goethes Werke*. Hamburger Ausgabe. Ed. Erich Trunz. München 1982–2008.

- *Sämtliche Werke. Briefe, Tagebücher und Gespräche*. Frankfurter Ausgabe. Ed. Hendrik Birus, et al. Frankfurt a. M. 1985ff.

- *Werke*. Berliner Ausgabe. Ed. Siegfried Seidel. Berlin 1960ff.

- *Goethes Briefe*. Hamburger Ausgabe. Ed. Karl Robert Mandelkow. München 1988.

- *Goethes Gespräche*. Ed. Woldemar Freiherr von Biedermann. Leipzig 1889–1896.

GOETHE, Johann Wolfgang von: *Goethe's Faust: Parts I and II*. Trans. Stuart Atkins. Princeton 2014.

HÖLDERLIN, Friedrich: *Sämtliche Werke*. Große Stuttgarter Ausgabe. Ed. Friedrich Beißner/Adolf Beck/Ute Oelmann. Stuttgart 1943–1985.

- *Hyperion and Selected Poems*. Ed. Eric L. Santner. New York 1990.

- *The Death of Empedocles. A Mourning-Play*. Trans. David F. Krell. New York 2008.

KLEIST, Heinrich von: *Sämtliche Werke und Briefe*. Brandenburger Ausgabe. Ed. Roland Reuß/Peter Staengle/Ingeborg Harms. Basel/Frankfurt a. M. 1988ff.

- »On the Marionette Theatre«. In: *The Drama Review: TDR*, Vol. 16, No. 3, The »Puppet« Issue (September 1972). Trans. Thomas G. Neumiller. 22–26.

Secondary Literature:

On Sloterdijk:
DOBENECK, Holger von: *Das Sloterdijk-Alphabet*: *Eine lexikalische Einführung in Sloterdijks Gedankenkosmos*. Würzburg 2006.

EVERS, Marco/Franke, Klaus/Grolle, Johann: »Zucht und deutsche Ordnung«. In: *Der Spiegel*, 39/1999, 300–316.

JÄGER, Lorenz: »Deutsches Beben. Ist die 'Kritische Theorie' am Ende? Zur Debatte um Peter Sloterdijk«. In: *Frankfurter Allgemeine Zeitung*, 09/13/1999.

JOHN, Matthias/VAN ZANTWIJK, Temilo: »Sloterdijk, der Humanismus und die Anthropologie des 18. Jahrhunderts«. In: Bernhard Kleeberg, et al. (Ed.): *Die List der Gene: Strategeme eines neuen Menschen*. Tübingen 2001. 171–189.

KOCH, Lars: »Sloterdijk-Debatte 2.0: 'Skandalöse' Anthropologie im diskursiven Spannungsfeld von Biotechnologie, Ökonomie und Zukunftsangst.« In: Kristin Bulkow & Christer Petersen (Ed.): *Skandale: Strukturen und Strategien öffentlicher Aufmerksamkeitserzeugung.* Wiesbaden 2011. 87–104.

Mohr, Reinhard: »Züchter des Übermenschen«. In: *Der Spiegel*, 36/1999. 268–171.

- »Der Herr Blasen«. In: *Der Spiegel*, 52/2002. 156–157.

Nennen, Heinz-Ulrich: *Philosophie in Echtzeit. Die Sloterdijk-Debatte*: *Chronik einer Inszenierung. Über Metaphernfolgenabschätzung, die Kunst des Zuschauers und die Pathologie der Diskurse.* Würzburg 2003.

Schinkel, Willem & Noordegraaf-Eelens, Liesbeth: »Peter Sloterdijk's Spherological Acrobatics: An Exercise in Introduction.« In: Willem Schinkel & Liesbeth Noordegraaf-Eelens (Ed.): *In Medias Res: Peter Sloterdijk's Spherological Poetics of Being.* Amsterdam 2011. 7–28.

Schmid, Sabine & Sloterdijk, Peter: »Anthropotechnik: Der Mensch gestaltet sich selbst«. In: *Das Magazin,* 11/2000.

Sloterdijk, Peter: *Selbstversuch ein Gespräch mit Carlos Oliviera.* München 1996.

- *Die Verachtung der Massen.* Frankfurt a. M. 2000.

- *Sphären III. Schäume.* Frankfurt a. M. 2004.

- »Die Revolution der gebenden Hand«. In: *Frankfurter Allgemeine Zeitung*, 23/2009. 23.

Tuinen, Sjoerd von: *Peter Sloterdijk. Ein Profil.* Paderborn 2007.

- »'Transgenous Philosophy': Posthumanism, Anthropotechnics and the Poetics of Natal Difference.« In: Willem Schinkel & Liesbeth Noordegraaf-Eelens (Ed.): *In Medias Res: Peter Sloterdijk's Spherological Poetics of Being.* Amsterdam 2011. 43–66.

On Campanella:

Bayertz, Kurt: *GenEthics: Technological Intervention in Human Reproduction as a Philosophical Problem.* Cambridge 1995.

Bublitz, Matthias: *Gegliederter Universalismus: Politische Philosophie und ihre Tendenzen in der bundesdeutschen Parteienprogrammatik.* Frankfurt a. M. 2010.

BRINKSCHRÖDER, Michael: *Sodom als Symptom. Gleichgeschlechtliche Sexualität Im Christlichen Imaginären – Eine Religionsgeschichtliche Anamnese.* Berlin 2006.

CHORDAS, Nina: *Forms in Early Modern Utopia: The Ethnography of Perfection.* Fernham 2010.

GERMANA, Ernst: »Tommaso Campanella. Die wissenschaftliche Revolution aus dem Kerker«. In: *Philosophen der Renaissance. Eine Einführung.* Ed. Paul Richard Blum. Darmstadt 1999. 222–236.

- *Tommaso Campanella. The Book and the Body of Nature.* Dordrecht 2010.

MAGGI, Armando: »Tommaso Campanella's Philosophy and the Birth of Modern Science«. In: *Modern Philology,* 3/2010. 475–492.

MALICH, Lisa: »Zeitpfeile, Zeitfaltung und Diskursanalyse: zu Kontinuitäten der Imaginationslehre«. In: *Berichte zur Wissenschaftsgeschichte,* 4/2011. 363–378.

STERNBERG, Kurt: »Über Campanellas ›Sonnenstaat‹«. In: *Historische Zeitschrift,* 3/1933. 520–570.

On Kant:

HEIDEGGER, Martin: *Kant und das Problem der Metaphysik.* Ed. Friedrich-Wilhelm von Herrmann. Frankfurt a. M. 1998.

HEIDEGGER, Martin: *Kant and the Problem of Metaphysics.* Trans. Richard Taft. Bloomington 1997.

HEITGER, Marian: »Aufklärung als pädagogisches Programm«. In: Lutz Koch/Christian Schönherr (Ed.): *Kant – Pädagogik und Politik.* Würzburg 2005. 133–143.

LOUDEN, Robert B.: *Kant's Impure Ethics: From Rational Beings to Human Beings.* New York 2000.

LÖWISCH, Dieter-Jürgen: »Immanuel Kant II«. In: *Pädagogisches Denken von den Anfängen bis zur Gegenwart.* Ed. Wolfgang Fischer & Dieter-Jürgen Löwisch. Darmstadt 1983. 140–153.

MESSER, August: *Kant als Erzieher.* Langensalza 1924.

RUHLOFF, Jörg: »Auch Moralisierung? Bemerkungen zur Aktualität von Kants Gliederung der Erziehungsaufgabe«. In: Lutz Koch/Christian Schönherr (Ed.): *Kant – Pädagogik und Politik.* Würzburg 2005. 23–33.

SURPRENANT, Chris W.: *Kant and the Cultivation of Virtue.* Abingdon 2014.

WISTUBA, Frank: »Kants Vorlesung über Pädagogik«. In: *Vierteljahresschrift für wissenschaftliche Pädagogik,* 83/2007. 470–477.

On Humboldt:

BORSCHE, Tilman: *Wilhelm von Humboldt.* München 1990.

FREESE, Rudolf: »Wilhelm von Humboldts Bildungs- und Humanitäts-idee«. In: Rudolf Hoberg (Ed.): *Sprache und Bildung. Beiträge zum 150. Todestag Wilhelm von Humboldts.* Darmstadt 1987. 13–52.

KAEHLER, Siegfried: *Wilhelm von Humboldt und der Staat.* Göttingen 1927.

ROSENFELD, Horst: »Universeller Bürger und Fachmann in Wilhelm von Humboldts ›Theorie der Bildung des Menschen‹«. In: Rudolf Hoberg (Ed.): *Sprache und Bildung. Beiträge zum 150. Todestag Wilhelm von Humboldts.* Darmstadt 1987. 307–323.

SCHULZE, Hagen: »Humboldt und das Paradox der Freiheit«. In: Bernfried Schlerath (Ed.): *Wilhelm von Humboldt. Vortragszyklus zum 150. Todestag.* Berlin/New York 1986. 145–168.

SPRANGER, Eduard: *Wilhelm von Humboldt und die Humanitätsidee.* Berlin 1909.

STEENBLOCK, Volker/LESSING, Hans-Ulrich (Ed.): *»Was den Menschen eigentlich zum Menschen macht . . . « – Klassische Texte einer Philosophie der Bildung.* Freiburg 2010.

VON HENTIG, Hartmut: *Bildung. Ein Essay.* München 1996.

WEBER, ERICH: *Pädagogik. Eine Einführung.* Donauwörth 1999.

On Key:

ANDRESEN, Sabine/Baader, Meike S.: *Wege aus dem Jahrhundert des Kindes – Tradition und Utopie bei Ellen Key.* Neuwied 1998.

ANDRESEN, Sabine/BAADER, Meike S./JACOBI, Juliane (Ed.): *Ellen Keys reformpädagogische Vision – »Das Jahrhundert des Kindes« und seine Wirkung.* Weinheim/Basel 2000.

BAADER, Meike S.: »Zur Konstruktion des Kindes in Ellen Keys Jahrhundert des Kindes. Das Jahrhundert des Kindes – am Ende? Ellen Key und der pädagogische Diskurs: eine Revision«. In: *Engagement. Zeitschrift für Erziehung und Schule,* 4/1998. 199-204.

FLITNER, Wilhelm & Kudritzki, Gerhard (Ed.): *Die Deutsche Reformpädagogik. Vol. I: Die Pioniere der pädagogischen Bewegung.* Düsseldorf/München 1961.

MANN, Katja: *Ellen Key. Ein Leben über die Pädagogik hinaus.* Darmstadt 2004.

RILKE, Rainer Maria: »Das Jahrhundert des Kindes«. In: Rilke: *Sämtliche Werke.* Wiesbaden/Frankfurt a. M. 1955–1966. Vol. 5. 584–592.

Rücker, Tobias: »Das Jahrhundert des Kindes? Ellen Key, die deutsche Pädagogik und die widersprüchliche Realität von Kindheit im 20.Jahrhundert«. In: Karl-Christoph Lingelbach/Hasko Zimmer (Ed.): *Jahrbuch für Pädagogik 1999. Das Jahrhundert des Kindes?*. Frankfurt a. M./Berlin/Bern/Bruxelles/New York/Wien 2000. 17–32.

On Goethe:

Adler, Jeremy: »Goethe's Use of Chemical Theory in his Elective Affinities«. In: Andrew Cunningham & Nicholas Jardine (Ed.): *Romanticism and the Sciences*. New York 1990. 263–279.

Arendt, Dieter: »Homunculus – der Geist ›in der Flasche‹ oder: ein mephistophelisches Märchen«. In: Sascha Feuchert et al. (Ed.): *Literatur und Geschichte. Festschrift für Erwin Leibfried*. Frankfurt a. M. 2007. 35–60.

Böhme, Gernot: *Faust als philosophischer Text*. Reutlingen 2005.

Buchwald, Reinhard: *Führer durch Goethes Faustdichtung. Erklärung des Werkes und Geschichte seiner Entstehung*. Stuttgart 1942.

Bub, Douglas F.: »The Crown Incident in the *Hexenküche*: A Reinterpretation«, in: *Modern Language Notes*, 3/1958. 200–206.

Ciupke, Markus: *Des Geklimpers vielverworrner Töne Rausch. Die metrische Gestaltung in Goethes »Faust«*. Göttingen 1994.

Drux, Rudolf: »Homunculus«. In: Günther Butzer/Joachim Jacob (Ed.): *Metzler Lexikon literarischer Symbole*. Stuttgart/Weimar 2008. 168–169.

● »Homunculus oder Leben aus der Retorte. Zur Kulturgeschichte eines literarischen Motivs seit Goethe«. In: Richard Görner (Ed.): *Tales from the Laboratory*. München 2005. 91–104.

Eckermann, Johann Peter: *Gespräche mit Goethe in den letzten Jahren seines Lebens*. Stuttgart 1998.

Emrich, Wilhelm: *Die Symbolik von Faust II. Sinn und Vorformen*. Berlin 1943.

Gaier, Ulrich: *Kommentar zu Goethes Faust*. Stuttgart 2002.

Hagen, Waltraud/Nahler, Edith (Ed.): *Quellen und Zeugnisse zur Druckgeschichte von Goethes Werken*. Bd. 1. Berlin 1966.

Horatschek, Annegreth: »Körper/Leib«. In: Ansgar Nünning (Ed.): *Metzler Lexikon Literatur- und Kulturtheorie*. 4. Ed. Stuttgart/Weimar 2008. 356.

Jessing, Benedikt: *Goethe*. Stuttgart/Weimar 1995.

KERÉNYI, Karl: »Das Ägäische Fest. Die Meeresgötterszene in Goethes Faust II (1941)«. In: Werner Keller (Ed.): *Aufsätze zu Goethes Faust II.* Darmstadt 1992. 160–189.

KORFF, Hermann August: *Faustischer Glaube. Versuch über das Problem humaner Lebenshaltung.* Leipzig 1938.

LANGE, Victor: »Faust. Der Tragödie Zweiter Teil«. In: Walter Hinderer (Ed.): *Goethes Dramen. Neue Interpretationen.* Stuttgart 1980. 281–312.

LATIMER, Dan: »Homunculus as Symbol: Semantic and Dramatic Functions of the Figure in Goethe's Faust«. In: *Modern Language Notes,* 89/1974. 812–820.

OSTEN, Manfred: *Homunculus, die beschleunigte Zeit und Max Beckmanns Illustrationen zur Modernität Goethes.* Mainz 2002.

- *»Alles veloziferisch« oder Goethes Entdeckung der Langsamkeit.* Frankfurt a. M. 2003.

On Hölderlin:

BLUMENBERG, Hans: »Wirklichkeitsbegriff und Möglichkeit des Romans« (1964). In: Hans Robert Jauß (Ed.): *Nachahmung und Illusion. Poetik und Hermeneutik 1.* München 1969. 9–27.

BRAUNGART, Wolfgang: »Hyperions Melancholie«. In: Valérie Lawitschka (Ed.): *Turm-Vorträge 1989/90/91. Hölderlin: Christentum und Antike.* Tübingen 1991. 111–140.

GAIER, Ulrich: »Hölderlins ›Hyperion‹: Compendium, Roman, Redex«. In: Ulrich Gaier/Michael Franz/Martin Vöhler (Ed.): *Hölderlin-Jahrbuch 21.* Eggingen 1978/79. 88–143.

- *Hölderlin. Eine Einführung.* Tübingen/Basel 1993.

HENRICH, Dieter: *Der Grund im Bewusstsein. Untersuchungen zu Hölderlins Denken (1794–1795).* Stuttgart 1992.

KREMER, Detlef: »Romantik«. In: Ansgar Nünning (Ed.): *Metzler Lexikon Literatur- und Kulturtheorien.* 4. Auflage. Stuttgart/Weimar 2008. 633–636.

THOMÄ, Dieter: »Ästhetisierung«. In: Volker Steenblock (Ed.): *Kolleg Praktische Philosophie.* Vol. 3. *Zeitdiagnose.* Stuttgart 2008. 133–167.

- *Erzähle dich selbst. Lebensgeschichte als philosophisches Problem.* Frankfurt a. M. 2007.

RAY, Hansjörg: »*Ohne Rückkehr*«. *Utopische Intention und poetischer Prozeß in Hölderlins Hyperion.* München 2003.

RYAN, Lawrence: »Hyperion«. In: Johann Kreuzer (Ed.): *Hölderlin-Handbuch.* Stuttgart/Weimar 2002. 176–197.

STIENING, Gideon: *Epistolare Subjektivität. Das Erzählsystem in Friedrich Hölderlins Briefroman »Hyperion oder Der Emerit in Griechenland«.* Tübingen 2005.

UERLINGS, Herbert (Ed.): *Theorie der Romantik.* Stuttgart 2009.

WEINBERG, Manfred: »Nächstens mehr. Erinnerung und Gedächtnis in Hölderlins *Hyperion*«. In: Günter Oesterle (Ed.): *Erinnern und Vergessen in der Europäischen Romantik.* Würzburg 2001. 97–117.

On Kleist:

BEIL, Ulrich Johannes: »Über das Marionettentheater«. In: Ingo Breuer (Ed.): *Kleist-Handbuch.* Stuttgart/Weimar 2009. 152–156.

- »Kenosis der idealistischen Ästhetik. Kleists *Über das Marionettentheater* als Schiller-reecriture«. In: *Kleist-Jahrbuch 2006.* Ed. Günter Blamberger/Gabriele Brandstetter/Ingo Breuer. Stuttgart/Weimar 2006. 75–99.

BLAMBERGER, Günter: »Von der Faszination riskanter Bewegungen. Anmerkungen zu Kleists Sportbetrachtungen«. In: *Kleist-Jahrbuch 2007.* 38–45.

GRIMM, Andrea: »Die Rede über den Körper. Zum Körperdiskurs in Kleists Texten ›Die Marquise von O....‹ und ›Über das Marionettentheater‹. In: Heinz Ludwig Arnold/Roland Reuss/Peter Staengle (Ed.): *Text und Kritik. Sonderband Heinrich von Kleist.* München 1993. 170–176.

KNAP, Janina: *Ästhetik der Anmut. Studien zur »Schönheit der Bewegung« im 18. Jahrhundert.* Frankfurt a. M. 1996.

KOSENINA, Alexander: »Anthropologie«. In: Ingo Breuer (Ed.): *Kleist-Handbuch.* Stuttgart/Weimar 2009. 243–246.

KUNZ, Josef: »Kleists Gespräch Über das Marionettentheater«. In: Müller-Seidel (Ed.): *Kleists Aufsatz über das Marionettentheater.* Berlin 1967. 76–88.

MÜLLER, Tim: *Der souveräne Mensch. Die Anthropologie Heinrich von Kleists.* Göttingen 2011.

OBERLIN, Gerhard: »Gott und Gliedermann. Das ›unendliche Objekt‹ in Heinrich von Kleists Erzählung ›Über das Marionettentheater‹ (1810)«. In: *Kleist-Jahrbuch 2007.* 272–288.

RIEGER, Stefan: »Choreographie und Regelung. Bewegungsfiguren nach Kleist Marionettentheater«. In: *Kleist-Jahrbuch 2007*. 162–182.

SCHEFELS, Klaus–Christoph: *Rückzug. Zur Negierung von Raum- und Körperordnungen im Werk Heinrich von Kleists*. Frankfurt a. M./Bern/New York 1986.

WIESE, Benno von: »Das verlorene und wieder zu findende Paradies. Eine Studie über den Begriff der Anmut bei Goethe, Kleist und Schiller«. In: Walter Müller-Seidel (Ed.): *Kleists Aufsatz über das Marionettentheater*. Berlin 1967. 196–221.

On Anthropotechnic/Anthropoetics:

BARKHOFF, Jürgen: »Perfecting Nature – Surpassing God: The Dream of Creating Artificial Humans around 1800«. In: Christian Emden & David R. Midgley (Ed.): *Science, Technology and German Cultural Imagination*. Bern 2005. 39–56.

BAUER-FUNKE, Cerstin & FEBEL, Gisele (Ed.): *Der automatisierte Körper. Literarische Visionen des künstlichen Menschen vom Mittelalter bis zum 21. Jahrhundert*. Berlin 2005.

BASHFORD, Alison & Levine, Philippa (Ed.): *The Oxford Handbook of the History of Eugenics*. New York 2010.

BAYERTZ, Kurt/SCHMIDT, Kurt W.: »»Es ist ziemlich teuer, authentisch zu sein…!‹ Von der ästhetischen Umgestaltung des menschlichen Körpers und der Integrität der menschlichen Natur«. In: Johann S. Ach & Arndt Pollmann (Ed.): *No Body is perfect. Baumaßnahmen am menschlichen Körper – Bioethische und ästhetische Aufrisse*. Bielefeld 2006. 43–62.

BREGER, Claudia/Krüger-Fürhoff, Irmela Marei/Nusser, Tanja (Ed.): *Engineering Life. Narrationen vom Menschen in Biomedizin, Kultur und Literatur*. Berlin 2008.

COENEN, Christopher/GAMMEL, Stefan/HEIL, Reinhard/WOYKE, Andreas (Ed.): *Die Debatte über »Human Enhancement«. Historische, philosophische und ethische Aspekte der technologischen Verbesserung des Menschen*. Bielefeld 2010.

CRABTREE, Pam J./ Campana, Douglas V./ Ryan, Kathleen (Ed.): *Early Animal Domestication and Its Cultural Context*. Philadelphia 1989.

DRUX, Rudolf (Ed.): *Die Geschöpfe des Prometheus – Der künstliche Mensch von der Antike bis zur Gegenwart*. Bielefeld 1994.

- »Maschinenmensch«. In: Günther Butzer & Joachim Jacob (Ed.): *Metzler Lexikon literarischer Symbole*. Stuttgart/Weimar 2008. 223–224.

ETKIND, Alexander: *Eros Of The Impossible: The History Of Psychoanalysis In Russia*. Trans. Noah & Maria Rubins. Boulder 1997.

FEBEL, Gisela (Ed.): *Menschenkonstruktionen. Künstliche Menschen in Literatur, Film, Theater und Kunst des 19. und 20. Jahrhunderts*. Göttingen 2004.

GEHRING, Petra: »Zwischen Menschenpark und Soft eugenics«. In: Petra Gehring (Ed.): W*as ist Biomacht? Vom zweifelhaften Mehrwert des Lebens*. Frankfurt a. M. 2006. 154-184.

GÖRNER, Rüdiger: »Prolegomena zu einer poetischen Kybernetik«. In: Rüdiger Görner (Ed.): *Tales from the Laboratory. Or, Homunculus Revisited*. München 2005. 7–30.

GREAT SOVIET ENCYCLOPEDIA. 65 vols. and one supplementary volume. 1st Ed. Moscow 1926–1933. Ed. by Soviet Encyclopedia, LLC., Vol. 3, 130–131.

GRIMM, Gunter E.: »›Elektronische Hirne‹. Zur literarischen Genese des Androiden«. In: *Literatur für Leser,* 2/1998. 73–90.

GRUEVSKA, Julia: »Kultur als 'ontische Notwendigkeit': Wilhelm Diltheys und Helmuth Plessners psychophysische Auffassung des Lebens.« In: Ralf Glitza & Kevin Liggieri (Ed.): *Kultur und Bildung. Die Geisteswissenschaften und der Zeitgeist des Naturalismus*. Freiburg i. Br. 2019. 52–66.

HAGEMEISTER, Michael/GROYS, Boris (Ed.): *Die neue Menschheit*. Frankfurt a. M. 2005.

HARTUNG, Gerald: *Philosophische Anthropologie*. Grundwissen Philosophie, 2. Ed., Stuttgart 2018.

HOYER, Klaus: *Exchanging human bodily material: Rethinking bodies and markets*. London 2013.

JUENGST, Eric T.: »Was bedeutet *Enhancement*?«. In: Bettina Schöne-Seifert & Davinia Talbot (Ed.): *Enhancement:* Paderborn 2009. 29–46.

MÜLLER, Oliver: *Zwischen Mensch und Maschine. Vom Glück und Unglück des Homo faber*. Frankfurt a. M. 2010.

LA METTRIE, Julien Offray De: *Machine Man and Other Writings*. Trans. and ed. Ann Thomson. New York 1996.

LIGGIERI, Kevin. »*Anthropotechnik«. Zur Geschichte eines umstrittenen Begriffs*. Göttingen 2020.

- »'[A]n der Front des Kampfes um den Menschen selbst'. Anthropogenetik und Anthropotechnik im sowjetischen Diskurs der 1920er Jahre«. In: *Berichte zur Wissenschaftsgeschichte*, 2/2016. 165–184.

- *Zur Domestikation des Menschen. Anthropotechnische und anthropoetische Optimierungsdiskurse.* Münster/Wien 2014.

PARACELSUS: »De generatione rerum naturalium«. In: Klaus Völker (Ed.): *Künstliche Menschen. Dichtungen und Dokumente über Golems, Homunculi, Androiden und liebende Statuen.* München 1971. 43–52.

ROTH, Volkbert M./BISCHOF, Paul (Ed.): *Leben ändern? Wir üben. Diskussion von Peter Sloterdijk 2009 über Anthropotechnik.* Sipplingen 2011.

SCHÖN, Erich: *Der Verlust der Sinnlichkeit oder die Verwandlung des Lesers.* Stuttgart 1987.

SCHERGER, Simone: »Die Kunst der Selbstgestaltung«. In: Barbara Becker & Irmela Schneider (Ed.): *Was vom Körper übrig bleibt. Körperlichkeit – Identität – Medien.* Frankfurt/New York 2000. 235–251.

SIEBEN, Anna/SABISCH-FECHTELPETER, Katja/STRAUB, Jürgen: »Menschen besser machen. Terminologische und theoretische Aspekte vielgestaltiger Optimierungen des Humanen«. In: Anna Sieben/Katja Sabisch-Fechtelpeter/Jürgen Straub (Ed.): *Menschen machen. Die hellen und dunklen Seiten humanwissenschaftlicher Optimierungsprogramme.* Bielefeld 2012. 27–79.

STRAUB, Jürgen: »Optimierungstypen. Ein provisorisches Nachwort zu Licht- und Schattenseiten von Menschenverbesserungs-programmen«. In: Anna Sieben/Katja Sabisch-Fechtelpeter/Jürgen Straub (Ed.): *Menschen machen. Die hellen und dunklen Seiten humanwissenschaftlicher Optimierungsprogramme.* Bielefeld 2012. 473–491.

TABBERT, Thomas T.: *Menschmaschinengötter. Künstliche Menschen in Literatur und Technik. Fallstudien einer Artifizialanthropologie.* Hamburg 2004.

TRAWNY, Peter: »Der Körper der Thersites und der Leib Christi. Zur Herkunft ethischer Probleme mit den neueren ›Anthropotechniken‹ im Rückgang auf Homer und Hegel«. In: Julia Jones (Ed.): *Mensch – Leben – Technik: Aktuelle Beiträge zur phänomenologischen Anthropologie.* Würzburg 2006. 101–117.

ZELLE, Carsten: »Maschinen-Metaphern in der Ästhetik des 18. Jahrhunderts (Lessing, Lenz, Schiller)«. In: *Zeitschrift für Germanistik*, 3/1997. 510–520.

ZONS, Rainer: »Die Machbarkeit des Menschen«. In: Mirhan Dabag & Kristin Platt (Ed.): *Die Machbarkeit der Welt. Wie der Mensch sich selbst als Subjekt der Geschichte entdeckt.* München 2006. 13–28.

Further Literature:

ADAS, Michael: *Machines as the Measure of Men.* Ithaca/London 2014.

AGAMBEN, Giorgio: *Homo Sacer. Sovereign Power and Bare Life.* Trans. Daniel Heller-Roazen. Stanford 1998.

AGAMBEN, Giorgio: *What is an Apparatus?: And Other Essays.* Trans. David Kishik & Stefan Pedatella. Stanford 2009.

ARENDT, Hannah: *Über die Revolution.* München 1994. 4. Ed.

BAILLIE, Harold W. & CASEY, Timothy K. (Ed.): *Is Human Nature Obsolete? Genetics, Bioengineering, and the Future of the Human Condition.* Cambridge 2004.

BAYERTZ, Kurt: »Darwinismus als Ideologie«. In: Kurt Bayertz/Bernhard Heidtmann/Hans-Jörg Rheinberger (Ed.): *Darwin und die Evolutionstheorie.* Köln 1982. 105–120.

BERGSTEDT, Bosse et al. (Ed.): *Tacit Dimensions of Pedagogy.* Münster 2012.

BOCK, Gisela: *Zwangssterilisation im Nationalismus. Studien zur Rassenpolitik und Frauenpolitik.* Opladen 1986.

BLUMENBERG, Hans: »Lebenswelt und Technisierung unter Aspekten der Phänomenologie« (1963). In: Hans Blumenberg: *Wirklichkeiten. In denen wir leben.* Stuttgart 1996. 7–64.

BOLZ, Norbert: *Das Gestell.* Paderborn 2012.

BOURDIEU, Pierre: *The Logic of Practice.* Trans. Richard Nice. New York 1990.

Bowen, James: *A History of Western Education.* London 2003.

BRAIDOTTI, Rosi: *The Posthuman.* Cambridge 2013.

- »Posthuman, All Too Human: Towards a New Process Ontology«. In: *Theory, Culture & Society*, 23/2006. 197–208.

BRANDT, Christina: »Die Diffusion des zukünftigen Menschen: Klonpraktiken und Visionen des Humanen, 1960-1980«. In: Florenze Vienne & Christina Brandt (Ed.): *Wissensobjekt Mensch. Humanwissenschaftliche Praktiken im 20. Jahrhundert.* Berlin 2008. 213–243.

BRÖCKLING, Ulrich et al. (Ed.): *Disziplinen des Lebens? Zwischen Anthropologie, Literatur und Politik.* Tübingen 2004.

- »Menschenökonomie, Humankapital. Eine Kritik der biopolitischen Ökonomie«. In: *Mittelweg, 36/2003.* 3–23.

BRÖCKLING, Ulrich/KRASSMANN, Susanne/LEMKE, Thomas (Ed.): *Gouvernementalität der Gegenwart. Studien zur Ökonomisierung des Sozialen.* Frankfurt a. M. 2000.

CAME, Daniel (Ed.): *Nietzsche on Art and Life.* New York 2014.

CANGUILHEM, Georges: *Knowledge of Life.* Trans. Stefanos Geroulanos & Daniela Ginsburg. New York 2008.

CHRISMAN, Oscar: *Paidologie. Entwurf zu einer Wissenschaft des Kindes.* Diss. phil. Jena 1896.

Clutton-Brock, Juliet: *A Natural History of Domesticated Mammals.* New York 1999.

COECKELBERGH, Mark: *New Romantic Cyborgs: Romanticism, Information Technology, and the End of the Machine.* Cambridge (MA) 2017.

DECROLY, Ovide: »Sociètè de Pèdotechnie«. In: *Die Experimentelle Pädagogik. Organ der Arbeitsgemeinschaft für experimentelle Pädagogik mit besonderer Berücksichtigung der experimentellen Didaktik und der Erziehung Schwachbegabter und abnormer Kinder.* Ed. Ernst Meumann, 4/1907. 255–256.

DELEUZE, Gillez/Guattari, Felix: *A Thousand Plateaus: Capitalism and Schizophrenia.* Trans. Brian Massumi. London 2005.

DEPAEPE, Marc/Simon, Frank/Herman, Frederik/Van Gorp, Angelo: »Brodskys hygienische Klappschulbank: Zu leicht für die schulische Mentalität«. In: Karin Priem/Gudrun M. König/Rita Casale (Ed.): *Zeitschrift für Pädagogik, 58. Beiheft: Die Materialität der Erziehung: Kulturelle und soziale Aspekte pädagogischer Objekte.* Weinheim 2012. 50–65.

Depaepe, Marc: *Zum Wohl des Kindes?: Pädologie, pädagogische Psychologie und experimentelle Pädagogik in Europa und den USA. 1890–1940,* Weinheim 1993, 173.

DESSAUER, Philipp: *Das binomische Geschichtsbild.* Freiburg im Breisgau 1946.

DEUBER-MANKOWSKY, Astrid: *Praktiken der Illusion – Kant, Nietzsche, Cohen, Benjamin bis Donna J. Haraway.* Berlin 2007.

DEUBER-MANKOWSKY, Astrid/HOLZHEY, Christoph F. E. (Ed.): *Situiertes Wissen und regionale Epistemologie. Zur Aktualität Georges Canguilhems und Donna J. Haraways.* Berlin/Wien 2013.

ENGLISH, Andrea R.: *Discontinuity in Learning: Dewey, Herbart and Education as Transformation*. Cambridge 2013.

ELIAS, Norbert: *Über den Prozess der Zivilisation*. Frankfurt a. M. 1997.

ENGELS, Eve-Maria: *Charles Darwin und seine Wirkung*. Frankfurt 2009.

FLUSSER, Vilém: »Gedächtnisse«. In: Ars electronica (Ed.): *Philosophien der neuen Technologie*. Berlin 1989. 41–55.

FOUCAULT, Michael: »Nietzsche, Genealogy, History«. In: Michel Foucault: *Language, Counter-Memory, Practice: Selected Essays and Interviews*. Ed. Donald F. Bouchard. Ithaca 1977. 139–164.

- *The History of Sexuality, vol. 1: The Will to Knowledge*. Trans. Robert Hurley. London 1998.

- *Der Wille zum Wissen. Sexualität und Wahrheit. Vol. 1*. Frankfurt a. M. 1977.

- »Body/Power«. In: *Power/Knowledge: Selected Interviews and Other Writings by Michel Foucault*. Ed. Colin Gordon. New York 1980. 55–62.

- »On the genealogy of ethics: an overview of work in progress«. In: Paul Rabinow (Ed.): *The Foucault Reader*. New York 1984.

- *Aesthetics, Method, and Epistemology: Essential Works of Foucault, 1954–1984*. Ed. James D. Faubion. New York 1998.

- *Discipline and Punish*. Trans. Alan Sheridan. New York 1995.

- *Ethics, Subjectivity, and Truth: Essential Works of Foucault, 1954–1984*. Ed. James D. Faubion. New York 1997.

- *Power: Essential Works of Foucault, 1954–1984*. Ed. James D. Faubion. New York 2000.

- *Technologies of the Self. A Seminar with Michel Foucault*. Ed. Patrick H. Hutton/Luther H. Martin/Huck Gutman. London 1988.

- *The Courage of Truth. The Government of Self and Others II: Lectures at the Collège de France 1983–1984*. Trans. Graham Burchell. New York 2011.

- *The History of Sexuality, vol. 2: The Use of Pleasure*. Trans. Robert Hurley. New York 1990.

- *The History of Sexuality, vol. 3: The Care of the Self*. Trans. Robert Hurley. New York 1988.

- *The Order of Things. An Archaeology of the Human Sciences*. London/New York 2004.

FUKUYAMA, Francis: *Our Posthuman Future: Consequences of the Biotechnology Revolution*. New York 2002.

GADAMER, Hans Georg: »Theorie, Technik, Praxis – die Aufgabe einer neuen Anthropologie«. In: Hans Georg Gadamer & Paul Vogler (Ed.): *Neue Anthropologie*. Bd. 1. *Biologische Anthropologie*. München 1972. S. IX–XXXVII.

GALTON, Francis: »Eugenics: Its definition, scope, and hope«. In: *The American Journal of Sociology*, 1/10 (1904). 43–51.

- »Hereditary Talent and Character«. In: *Macmillan's Magazine* 12/1865. 157–166; 318–327.

- *Hereditary Genius: An Inquiry Into Its Laws and Consequences*. London 1892.

GAO, Quang: »Bourdieu and Body«. In: Lisa Hunter/Wayne Smith/Elke Emerald (Ed.): *Pierre Bourdieu and Physical Culture*. London/New York 2015. 143–148.

GEHLEN, Arnold: *Der Mensch*. 13th Ed. Wiesbaden 1986.

GEHRING, Petra: »Biologische Politik um 1900. Reform, Therapie, Experiment?«. In: Birgit Griesecke/Marcus Krause/Nicolas Pethes/Katja Sabisch (Ed.): *Kulturgeschichte des Menschenversuchs im 20. Jahrhundert*. Frankfurt a. M. 2009. 48–77.

GLASER, Horst Albert & Rossbach, Sabine: *The Artificial Human*. Frankfurt a. M./Bern/New York 2011.

HARAWAY, Donna: »The Biopolitics of Postmodern Bodies: Determinations of Self in Immune System Discourse«. In: Janet Price & Margrit Shildrick (Ed.): *Feminist Theory and the Body: A Reader*. New York 1999. 203–214.

- *Simians, Cyborgs and Women: The Reinvention of Nature*. New York 1991.

Hardt, Michael & Negri, Antonio: *Empire*. Cambridge (MA) 2000.

HAECKEL, Ernst: *Die Lebenswunder* (1904). Stuttgart 1923.

HAUSKELLER, Michael: *Biotechnology and the Integrity of Life: Taking Public Fears Seriously*. New York 2016.

Hayles, Katherine: *How We Became Posthuman: Virtual Bodies in Cybernetics, Literature, and Informatics*. Chicago 1999.

HEGEL, Georg Wilhelm Friedrich: *Vorlesungen über die Ästhetik III*. Theorie-Werk-Ausgabe. Vol. 15. Frankfurt a. M. 1970.

HERDER, Johann Gottfried Herder: *Abhandlung über den Ursprung der Sprache*. Stuttgart 1993.

HÖRL, Erich: »Die offene Maschine. Heidegger, Günther und Simondon über die technologische Bedingung«. In: *Modern Language Notes*, 23/2008. 632–655.

- »Die Technologische Bedingung. Zur Einführung«. In: Erich Hörl (Ed.): *Die technologische Bedingung. Zur Einführung*. Frankfurt a. M. 2011. 7–53.

HÖRL, Erich & HAGNER, Michael (Ed.): *Die Transformationen des Humanen. Beiträge zur Kulturgeschichte der Kybernetik*. Frankfurt a. M. 2008.

HÖRNER, Wolfgang/DRINK, Barbara/JOBST, Solvejg: *Bildung, Erziehung, Sozialisation*. Opladen 2008.

HUI, YUK: *On the Existence of Digital Objects*. Minneapolis 2016.

HUSSERL, Edmund: *Gesammelte Werke*. Husserliana. Den Haag 1950ff. Vol. 2.

HUXLEY, Julian: »Transhumanism«. In: Julian Huxley (Ed.): *New Bottles for New Wine. Essays*. London 1957. 13–17.

JACOB, François: *Of Flies, Mice, and Men*. Trans. Giselle Weiss. Cambridge (MA) 1998.

JACOBI, Friedrich Heinrich: »Etwas, das Lessing gesagt hat. ein Commentar zu den Reisen der Päpste«. In: Jacobi: *Werke*. Leipzig 1815. Vol. 2. 325–389.

JARVIS, Peter & Watts, Mary (Ed.): *The Routledge International Handbook of Learning*. London 2012.

JOHNSON, Dominic: *The Art of Living: An Oral History of Performance Art*. London 2015.

JONAS, Hans: »Philosophical Reflections on Experimenting with Human Subjects«. In: *Daedalus*, 98/1969. 219–246.

Kang, Minsoo: *Sublime Dreams of Living Machines*. Cambridge/London 2011.

Karafyllis, Nicole C.: »Biofakte – Grundlagen, Probleme, Perspektiven«. In: *Erwägen Wissen Ethik*, 17/2006. 547–558

  • »Ethical and epistemological problems of hybridizing living beings: Biofacts and Body Shopping«. In: Wenchao Li & Hans Poser (Ed.): *Ethical Considerations on Today's Science and Technology. A German–Chinese Approach*. Münster 2008. 185–198.

Kelle, Helga: »Kinder in der Schule. Zum Zusammenhang von Schuldpädagogik und Kindheitsforschung«. In: Georg Breidenstein & Annedore Prengel (Ed.): *Schulforschung und Kindheitsforschung – Ein Gegensatz*. Wiesbaden 2005. 139–160.

Kevles, Daniel J.: *In the Name of Eugenics: Genetics and the Uses of Human Heredity*. New York 1985.

Knud Illeris: »An Overview of the History of Learning Theory«. In: *European Journal of Education*, 53/2018. 86–101.

Kohut, Heinz: *Die Heilung des Selbst*. Frankfurt a. M. 1981.

Krajewski, Markus: *The Server. A Media History from the Present to the Baroque*. Trans. Ilinca Iurascu. New Haven/London 2018.

Kraus, Anja: »Gender, the postmodern paradigm shift and Pedagogical Anthropology«. In: Carol A. Taylor et al. (Ed.): *Gender in Learning and Teaching: Feminist Dialogues Across International Boundaries*. Abingdon 2019. 54–67.

Lahmann, Heinrich: *Die diätische Blutmischung (Dysämie) als Grundursache aller Krankheiten. Ein Beitrag zur Lehre von der Krankheitsdisposition und Krankheitsverhütung*. Leipzig 1894.

Latour, Bruno/Woolgar, Steve: *Laboratory Life. The Construction of Scientific Facts*. New Jersey 1986.

Latour, Bruno: *We have never been modern*. Trans. Catherine Porter. Cambridge (MA) 1993.

Lederberg, Joshua: »Die biologische Zukunft des Menschen«. In: Robert Jungk/Hans-Josef Mundt (Ed.): *Das umstrittene Experiment: Der Mensch*. München 1966. 292–301.

Lemke, Thomas: *Gouvernementalität und Biopolitik*. Wiesbaden 2007.

Lepenies, Wolf: »Probleme einer historischen Anthropologie«. In: Reinhard Rürup (Ed.): *Historische Sozialwissenschaft. Beiträge zur Einführung in die Forschungspraxis*. Göttingen 1977. 126–159.

Lepenies, Wolf: »Naturgeschichte und Anthropologie im 18. Jahrhundert«. In: Bernhard Fabian/Wilhelm Schmidt-Biggemann/Rudolf Vierhaus (Ed.): *Deutschlands kulturelle Entfaltung – Die Neubestimmung des Menschen.* München 1980. 211–226.

Liggieri, Kevin: »Julien Offray de La Mettrie. Mr. Machine? – Mehr als Maschine«. In: Kevin Liggieri (Ed.): *Bad Boys der Philosophie.* Würzburg 2014.

- »Wir sind zur Selbstformung verdammt. Wilhelm Schmid und seine Philosophie der Lebenskunst«. In: *Zeitschrift für Didaktik der Philosophie und Ethik (ZDPE)*, 1/2014.

- »Ich nahm mich selbst in die Hand. Die Lebenskunst Nietzsches als Selbsttechnik bei Michael Foucault und Peter Sloterdijk«. In: *Nietzscheforschung 21.* Ed. Renate Reschke/Nikos Loukidelis/Günter Gödde. Halle an der Saale 2014.

Lorenz, Konrad: »Psychologie und Stammesgeschichte« (1954). In: Konrad Lorenz: *Über tierisches und menschliches Verhalten. Aus dem Werdegang der Verhaltenslehre.* München 1965, Vol. 2. 201–255.

Löbl, Rudolf: *Texnh–Techne. Untersuchungen zur Bedeutung dieses Worts in der Zeit von Homer bis Aristoteles.* Vol. 1: *Von Homer bis zu den Sophisten,* Würzburg 1997. Vol. 2: *Von den Sophisten bis Aristoteles.* Würzburg 2003.

Löbsack, Theo: *Die Biologie und der liebe Gott. Aspekte einer zukunftsreichen Wissenschaft.* München 1969.

Löwisch, Dieter-Jürgen: »Immanuel Kant II«. In: *Pädagogisches Denken von den Anfängen bis zur Gegenwart.* Ed. Wolfgang Fischer & Dieter-Jürgen Löwisch. Darmstadt 1983.

Luhmann, Niklas: *Schriften zur Kunst und Literatur.* Ed. Niels Werber. Frankfurt a. M. 2008.

Lyotard, Jean-François: *The Postmodern Condition: A Report on Knowledge.* Trans. Geoff Bennington & Brian Massumi. Minneapolis 1984.

Lysemose, Kasper: »The Being, the Origin and the Becoming of Man: A Presentation of Philosophical Anthropogenealogy and Some Ensuing Methdodological Considerations«. In: *Human Studies,* 35/2012. 115–130.

Meloni, Maurizio: *Political Biology: Science and Social Values in Human Heredity from Eugenics to Epigenetics.* New York 2012.

MELZER, Sara E. & Norberg, Kathryn (Ed.): *From the Royal to the Republican Body: Incorporating the Political in Seventeenth and Eighteenth-Century France*. Berkeley 1998.

Mendieta, Eduardo: »Life«. In: Leonard Lawlor & John Nale (Ed.): *The Cambridge Foucault Lexicon*. New York 2014. 254–262.

Meumann, Ernst: »Experimentelle Pädagogik und Schulreform«. In: *Zeitschrift für Pädagogische Psychologie*, 12/1911. 1–13.

Meumann, Ernst: *Vorlesungen zur Einführung in die Experimentelle Pädagogik und ihre psychologischen Grundlagen* (Vol. 1, second edition). Leipzig 1911.

MEYER-DRAWE, Käte: *Menschen im Spiegel ihrer Maschinen*. München 1996.

- »Von der Marionette bis zum autopoietischen System. Maschinenbilder in der Pädagogik«. In: *Vierteljahrsschrift für wissenschaftliche Pädagogik*, 4/1995. 358-373.

- »Mensch und Maschine. Nachdenkliches zu neuzeitlichen Selbstkonzeptionen des Menschen«. In: Jörg Ruhloff & Klaus, Schaller (Ed.): *Pädagogische Einsätze 1991. Festschrift für Theodor Ballauff zum 80. Geburtstag*. Sankt Augustin 1991. 121-128.

- »Maschine«. In: Christoph Wulf (Ed.): *Vom Menschen. Handbuch Historische Anthropologie*. Weinheim/Basel 1997. 726–738.

- »Education«. In: Lester Embree et al. (Ed.): *Encyclopedia of Phenomenology*. Dordrecht 1997. 157–162.

- »Töten aus Barmherzigkeit? Biopolitische Tendenzen der Lebensreformbewegung. Erich Christian Schröder zum 80. Geburtstag«. In: Käte Meyer-Drawe & Kristin Platt (Ed.): *Wissenschaft im Einsatz*. München 2007. 205–217.

- *Diskurse des Lernens*. Paderborn 2012.

MIRANDOLA, Giovanni Pico della: *Über die Würde des Menschen*. Hamburg 1990.

MORAVEC, Hans: Robot: *Mere Machine to Transcendent Mind*. Oxford 2000.

MORGENSTERN, Christian: *Stufen. Eine Entwickelung in Aphorismen und Tagebuch-Notizen*. München 1922.

MÖHRING, Maren: »Thermodynamik und Freikörperkultur. Praxis des Lichtluftbades«. In: Florenze Vienne & Christina Brandt (Ed.): *Wissensobjekt Mensch. Humanwissenschaftliche Praktiken im 20. Jahrhundert*. Berlin 2008. 89–111.

MÜLLER, Heiner: *Jenseits der Nation*. Berlin 1991.

MÜLLER-WILLE, Staffan & Christina Brandt (Ed.): *Heredity Explored: Between Public Domain and Experimental Science, 1850–1930*. Cambridge 2016.

MUCHEMBLED, Michael: *Die Erfindung des modernen Menschen. Gefühlsdifferenzierung und kollektive Verhaltensweisen des Absolutismus*. Hamburg 1990.

NEHAMAS, Alexander: *Nietzsche: Life as Literature*. London 1985.

NIETZSCHE, Friedrich: *Werke. Kritische Studienausgabe*. Ed. Giorgio Colli & Mazzino Montinari. Berlin/New York 1967ff.

- *Beyond Good and Evil: Prelude to a Philosophy of the Future*. Trans. Judith Norman. Ed. Rolf-Peter Horstmann. New York 2002.

- *Daybreak: Thoughts on the Prejudices of Morality*. Ed. Maudemarie Clark & Brian Leiter. Trans. R. J. Hollingdale. New York 1997.

- *The Genealogy of Morality*. Trans. Carol Diethe. New York 2006.

- *Thus Spoke Zarathustra*. Trans. Adrian Del Caro & Robert Pippin. New York 2006.

NOVALIS: *Schriften. Die Werke Friedrich von Hardenbergs*. Historischkritische Ausgabe. Ed. Richard Samuel. Stuttgart 1960ff.

NYNS, Arthur: »La pédotechnie«. In: *Zuid en Noord*, 1/1910. 469–482.

OVERHAGE, Paul: *Experiment Menschheit. Die Steuerung der menschlichen Evolution*. Frankfurt a. M. 1967.

PAGEL, Julius: »Über den Versuch am lebenden Menschen«. In: *Deutsche Aerzte-Zeitung*, 10/1905. 217–228.

PATTON, Paul: »Technology (of Discipline, Governmentality, and Ethics)«. In: Leonard Lawlor & John Nale (Ed.): *The Cambridge Foucault Lexicon*. New York 2014. 503–508.

PETHES, Nicolas: »Die Topik des Unvorstellbaren«. In: Nicolas Pethes & Sandra Richter (Ed.): *Medizinische Schreibweisen. Ausdifferenzierung und Transfer zwischen Medizin und Literatur (1600-1900)*. Tübingen 2008. 321-333.

PETHES, Nicolas & KRAUSE, Marcus (Ed.): *Literarische Experimentalkulturen. Poetologien des Experiments im 19. Jahrhundert.* Würzburg 2005.

PLESSNER, Helmut: *Die Stufen des Organischen und der Mensch. Einleitung in die philosophische Anthropologie* (1928). Berlin/New York 1975.

- »Zur Anthropologie des Schauspielers« (1948). In: Helmuth Plessner: *Ausdruck und menschliche Natur.* Frankfurt a. M. 2003. 399–418.

- *Levels of Organic Life and the Human: An Introduction to Philosophical Anthropology.* Trans. Millay Hyatt. New York 2019.

- *Philosophische Anthropologie.* Ed. Julia Gruevska/Hans-Ulrich Lessing/Kevin Liggieri. Berlin 2019.

PLOETZ, Alfred: *Die Tüchtigkeit unserer Rasse und der Schutz der Schwachen. Ein Versuch über Rassenhygiene und ihr Verhältnis zu den humanen Idealen, besonders zum Socialismus. Grundlinien einer Rassen-Hygiene, 1. Theil.* Berlin 1895.

- »Die Begriffe Rasse und Gesellschaft und einige damit zusammenhängende Probleme«. In: Deutsche Gesellschaft für Soziologie (Ed.): *Verhandlungen des Ersten Deutschen Soziologentages (vom 19.–22. Oktober 1910 in Frankfurt).* Tübingen 1911. 111–136.

PLUMPE, Gerhard/WERBER, Niels: »Literatur ist codierbar. Aspekte einer systemtheoretischen Literaturwissenschaft«. In: Siegfried J. Schmidt (Ed.): *Literaturwissenschaft und Systemtheorie. Positionen, Kontroversen, Perspektiven.* Opladen 1993. 9–44.

PUDOR, Heinrich: *Die neue Erziehung. Essays über die Erziehung zur Kunst und zum Leben.* Leipzig 1902.

PROBST, Paul & Bringmann, Wolfgang G.: »Ernst Meumann and William Stern: Analyse ihres Wirkens in Hamburg (1910–1933) unter Berücksichtigung biographischer und soziokultureller Hintergründe«. In: *Geschichte der Psychologie,* 19/1993. 1–14.

Querton, Louis: »L'Organisation du controle du développement de l'enfant«. In: *Ioteyko,* 2/1912. 105–111.

REICHENBACH, Roland: »›La fatigue de soi‹. Bemerkungen zu einer Pädagogik der Selbstsorge«. In: Norbert Ricken & Markus Rieger-Ladich (Ed.): *Michel Foucault. Pädagogische Lektüren.* Wiesbaden. 187–200.

RHEINBERGER, Hans-Jörg/MÜLLER-WILLE, Staffan: *Vererbung. Geschichte und Kultur eines biologischen Konzepts.* Frankfurt a. M. 2009.
RHEINBERGER, Hans-Jörg/MÜLLER-WILLE (Ed.): *Heredity Produced: At the Crossroads of Biology, Politics an Culture, 1500–1870.* New York 2007.

- »Technische Reproduzierbarkeit organischer Natur – aus der Perspektive einer Geschichte der Molekularbiologie«. In: Martin G. Weiß (Ed.): *Bios und Zoe. Die menschliche Natur im Zeitalter ihrer technischen Reproduzierbarkeit.* Frankfurt a. M. 2009. 11–33.

RHEINBERGER, Hans-Jörg & MÜLLER-WILLE, Staffan. *A Cultural History of Heredity.* Chicago 2012.
RHEINBERGER, Hans-Jörg: *An Epistemology of the Concrete: Twentieth-Century Histories of Life.* Durham/London 2010.
RHEINBERGER, Hans-Jörg: *Toward a history of epistemic things: Synthesizing proteins in the test tube.* Stanford 1997.
RITTER, Joachim et al.: »Technik«. In: *Historisches Wörterbuch der Philosophie.* Ed. Joachim Ritter & Karlfried Gründer. Vol. 10. Basel 1998. 940–952.
ROHLEDER, Hermann: *Die Zeugung beim Menschen. Eine sexualpathologische Studie aus der Praxis. Mit Anhang: Die künstliche Zeugung (Befruchtung) beim Menschen.* Leipzig 1911.

- »Der heutige Stand der Eugenik«. In: *Zeitschrift für Sexualwissenschaften,* 2/1915. 17–28.

ROSE, Nikolas: *The Politics of Life Itself. Biomedicine, Power, and Subjectivity in the Twenty-First Century.* Princeton 2006.

- »Neurochemical selves«. In: *Society,* 41/November/December 2003. 46–59.

RUSSEL, Nicholas: *Like Engend'ring Like. Heredity and Animal Breeding in Early Moderne England.* Cambridge 1986.
SARASIN, Philipp: »Die Geschichte der Gesundheitsvorsorge. Das Verhältnis von Selbstsorge und staatlicher Intervention im 19. und 20. Jahrhundert«. In: *Cardiovascular Medicine,* 14/2 (2011). 41–45.

- »Feind im Blut: Die Bedeutung des Blutes in der deutschen Bakteriologie, 1870–1900«. In: Christina von Braun (Ed.): *Mythen des Blutes.* Frankfurt a. M. 2007. 296–310.

- »Foucault, Burckhard, Nietzsche und die Hygieniker«. In: Jürgen Martuschkat (Ed.): *Geschichte schreiben mit Foucault*. Frankfurt a. M./New York 2002. 195–218.

- *Reizbare Maschinen – eine Geschichte des Körpers 1765–1914*. Frankfurt a. M. 2001.

SCHILLER, Friedrich: *Werke*. Nationalausgabe. Ed. Julius Petersen & Friedrich Beissner. Weimar 1943ff.

SCHILLER, Friedrich: *On the Aesthetic Education of Man*. Trans. Reginald Snell. Mineola/New York 2004.

SCHLEGEL, Friedrich: *Kritische-Friedrich-Schlegel-Ausgabe*. Ed. Ernst Behler et al. Paderborn 1958ff.

SCHMID, Wilhelm: *Auf der Suche nach einer neuen Lebenskunst*. Frankfurt a. M. 2000.

- *Philosophie der Lebenskunst*. Frankfurt a. M. 1998.

- »Über den Versuch zur Neubegründung einer Philosophie der Lebenskunst«. In: Volker Steenblock (Ed.): *Kolleg Praktische Philosophie*. Bd. 3. *Zeitdiagnose*. Stuttgart 2008. 240–270.

SCHMIDGEN, Henning: »Fehlformen des Wissens«. In: Georges Canguilhem: *Die Herausbildung des Reflexbegriffes im 17. und 18. Jahrhundert*. Trans. Henning Schmidgen. München 2008. VII–LVIII.

SCHMITZ-EMANS, Monika: »Der Maschinenmensch als Spiegelbild der Menschenmaschine. Zur Verwertung des Automatenmotivs durch Jean Paul«. In: Horst Albert Glaser & Wolfgang Kaempfer (Ed.): *Maschinenmenschen. Referate der Triestiner Tagung*. Frankfurt a. M./Bern/New York/Paris 1988. 97–123.

Schroeder, H.: *Die Gesunderhaltung in der Ehe*. 5. Ed. Leipzig 1984.

Schui, Florian: Rebellious Prussians: *Urban Political Culture under Frederick the Great and his Successors*. Oxford 2013. 176–194.

Serpell, James (Ed.): *The Domestic Dog: Its Evolution, Behaviour and Interactions with People*. New York 2002.

SIMONDON, Gilbert: *On the Mode of Existence of Technical Objects*. Trans. Cecile Malaspina & John Rogove. Washington 2017.

SIMONS, Maarten: »Lernen, Leben und Investieren: Anmerkungen zur Biopolitik«. In: Norbert Ricken & Markus Rieger-Ladisch (Ed.): *Michel Foucault: Pädagogische Lektüren*. Wiesbaden 2004. 165–185

SLUYS, Alexis: *L'Evolution de la pédagogie*. Geneva 1911.

SMELTEN, Nicolas: »Pédotechnie«. In: *Zuid en Noord*, 1/1910. 110–113.

SPENGLER, Oswald: *Der Untergang des Abendlandes*. München 1923.

STAGL, Justin/REINHARD, Wolfgang: »Einleitung«. In: Justin Stagl & Wolfgang Reinhard (Ed.): *Grenzen des Menschseins – Probleme einer Definition des Menschlichen*. Wien/Köln/Weimar 2005. 9–33.

STERN, William: *Person und Sache. System des kritischen Personalismus. Zweiter Band: Die menschliche Persönlichkeit*. Leipzig 1918.

STOFF, Heiko: »Eine Geschichte der Dinge und eine dingliche Geschichte des Menschen. Methodische Probleme«. In: Florenze Vienne & Christina Brandt (Ed.): *Wissensobjekt Mensch. Humanwissenschaftliche Praktiken im 20. Jahrhundert*. Berlin 2008. 43–67.

OJAKANGAS, Mika: *On the Greek Origins of Biopolitics: A Reinterpretation of the History of biopower*. London/New York 2016.

ULLERSPERGER, Johann Baptist: »Pädiotrophie, Pädiopathieen und Pädiatrik im Allgemeinen und in ihrem richtigen Verhältnisse zur Morbilität und Mortalität der Neugeborenen, der Säuglinge und der Kinder in den ersten Lebensjahren«. In: *Journal für Kinderkrankheiten*, 49/1867. Ed. Friedrich Jacob Behrend. 1–132.

UNGEWITTER, Richard: *Kultur und Nacktheit. Eine Forderung von Richard Ungewitter*. Stuttgart 1911.

URAY, Johannes: *Die Wöhlersche Harnstoffsynthese und das wissenschaftliche Weltbild, Analyse eines Mythos*. Graz 2009.

VAUCANSON, Jacques de: *Beschreibung eines mechanischen Kunst-Stucks, und Automatischen Flöten-Spielers, so denen Herren von der Königlichen Academie der Wissenschaften zu Paris durch den Herrn Vaucanson Erfinder dieser Maschine überreicht worden*. Augsburg 1748.

VIENNE, Florenze: »Gestörtes Zeugungsvermögen: Samenzellen als neues humanmedizinisches Objekt, 1895–1945«. In: Florenze Vienne & Christina Brandt (Ed.): *Wissensobjekt Mensch. Humanwissenschaftliche Praktiken im 20. Jahrhundert*. Berlin 2008. 165–187.

VON VERSCHUER, Otmar: *Rassenhygiene als Wissenschaft und Staatsaufgabe*. Frankfurt a. M. 1936.

VOGLER, Paul: »Disziplinärer Methodenkontext und Menschenbild«. In: Hans Georg Gadamer & Paul Vogler (Ed.): *Neue Anthropologie*. Vol. 1. *Biologische Anthropologie*. München 1972. 3–22.

VÖLKER, Klaus (Ed.): *Künstliche Menschen*. Frankfurt a. M. 1994.

WAGNER, Friedrich: »Die Manipulierung des Menschen durch Genwissenschaft. Geschichte, Methoden, Ziele und Folgen«. In: Friedrich Wagner (Ed.): *Menschenzüchtung. Das Problem der genetischen Manipulation des Menschen*. München 1969. 13–49.

WALLACH, Otto: *Briefwechsel zwischen J. Berzelius und F. Wöhler im Auftrage der Königl. Gesellschaft der Wissenschaften zu Göttingen*. Leipzig 1901. Vol. 1.

WAWRZYN, Lienhard: *Der Automaten-Mensch. E.T.A. Hoffmanns Erzählungen vom »Sandmann«*. Berlin 1976.

WEISS, Martin G.: »Die Auflösung der menschlichen Natur«. In: Martin G. Weiß (Ed.): *Bios und Zoe. Die menschliche Natur im Zeitalter ihrer technischen Reproduzierbarkeit*. Frankfurt a. M. 2009. 35–54.

WELCH, Rhiannon Noel: *Vital Subjects: Race and Biopolitics in Italy*. Liverpool 2016.

WIESER, Wolfgang: »Einleitung. Das umstrittene Experiment: Der Mensch – Grenzen und Möglichkeiten wissenschaftlicher Prognosen«. In: Robert Jung & Hans Josef Mundt (Ed.): *Das umstrittene Experiment: Der Mensch*. München 1966. 9–10.

ZONS, Rainer: »Die Machbarkeit des Menschen«. In Mirhan Dabag & Kristin Platt (Ed.): *Die Machbarkeit der Welt. Wie der Mensch sich selbst als Subjekt der Geschichte entdeckt*. München 2006. 13–28.

Internet:

BRAUNGART, Wolfgang: Hyperions Melancholie. (07/14/2005). In: Goethezeitportal. http://www.goethezeitportal.de/db/wiss/hoelderlin/hyperion_braungart.pdf (02/24/2020).

DE SAINT EXUPÉRY, Antoine: The Little Prince 62 https://archive.org/details/TheLittlePrince_201603 (02/23/2020).

LIESSMANN, Konrad Paul: Sloterdijk ist sicherlich kein Kryptofaschist. Über den Menschen im Zeitalter seiner technischen Reproduzierbarkeit. In: *Profil*, Heft 41. www.musgym.salzburg.at/Media/GenetikL.doc (02/24/2020).

SLOTERDIJK, Peter: »Optimierung des Menschen«. (12/06/2005) https://www.youtube.com/watch?v=YJ73FZBI6L8 (02/24/2020).

Hermeneutics and Anthropology / Hermeneutik und Anthropologie

Prof. Dr. Andrea Marlen Esser (Universität Jena), Prof. Dr. Armin Grunwald (Karslruhe Institute of Technology – KIT) und Prof. Dr. Dr. Mathias Gutmann (Karslruhe Institute of Technology – KIT)

Michael Decker; Mathias Gutmann; Julia Knifka (Eds.)
Evolutionary Robotics, Organic Computing and Adaptive Ambience
Epistemological and ethical implications of technomorphic descriptions of technologies
The central features and performances of technologies are often referred to as if they were living entities, thus they are supposed to act as human agents, simulate human activities, properties or skills. Technomorphic and biomorphic descriptions are not only present in everyday language use, but within the sciences as well.
In this book, the authors reflect on the methodological, anthropological as well as normative roles metaphors play in the development and implementation of adaptive and intelligent technologies.
The structures, areas of applications and implications of technomorphic and biomorphic descriptions are put under scrutiny in order to provide guiding knowledge for technology developers and policy makers and initiate critical refelctions of exposure to new technologies.
Bd. 6, 2015, 224 S., 59,90 €, br., ISBN 978-3-643-90151-4

Knud Böhle; Jochen Berendes; Mathias Gutmann; Caroline Robertson-von Trotha; Constanze Scherz (Hg.)
Computertechnik und Sterbekultur
Die Beiträge des Buches geben einen Einblick, wie das Sterben und das Weiterleben nach dem Tod – zumindest in der Erinnerung und in den Medien – fortschreitend und tiefgreifend durch den Einsatz von Techniken verändert werden.
Die Vielfalt der dargebotenen Perspektiven aus Informatik, Philosophie, Kulturwissenschaft, Kunstgeschichte, Medienwissenschaft, Literaturwissenschaft, Religionswissenschaft, Soziologie, Technikfolgenabschätzung und Theologie macht die Produktivität einer interdisziplinären Thanatologie deutlich.
Bd. 5, 2014, 272 S., 24,90 €, br., ISBN 978-3-643-11071-8

Benjamin Rathgeber
Modellbildung in den Kognitionswissenschaften
Bd. 4, 2011, 304 S., 29,90 €, br., ISBN 978-3-643-10890-6

Michael Decker; Mathias Gutmann (Eds.)
Robo- and Informationethics
Some Fundamentals
Bd. 3, 2012, 264 S., 29,90 €, br., ISBN 978-3-643-90208-5

René Thun
Freiheit und Methode
Bd. 2, 2008, 232 S., 24,90 €, br., ISBN 978-3-8258-0349-0

Michael Bölker; Mathias Gutmann; Wolfgang Hesse (Hg.)
Menschenbilder und Metaphern im Informationszeitalter
Bd. 1, 2010, 288 S., 29,90 €, br., ISBN 978-3-643-10310-9

LIT Verlag Berlin – Münster – Wien – Zürich – London
Auslieferung Deutschland / Österreich / Schweiz: siehe Impressumsseite

Ethik in der Praxis/Practical Ethics
Studien/Studies
Ilhan Ilkilic (Universität Istanbul), Arnd T. May (Erfurt), Amir Muzur (Universität Rijeka),
Hans-Martin Sass (Universität Bochum/Georgetown University Washington), Martin Woesler
(Universität Witten/Herdecke)

Arnd T. May; Barbara Seehase
Advance Care Planning (ACP) in der Eingliederungshilfe
Grundlagen und Praxis zur gesundheitlichen Versorgungsplanung (SGB V §132 g)
Bd. 44, 2020, ca. 120 S., ca. 39,00 €, br., ISBN 978-3-643-14292-4

Iva Rinčić; Amir Muzur
Fritz Jahr and the Emergence of European Bioethics
The book presents the results of a long research into the life and work of the German theologian and
teacher Fritz Jahr (1895 – 1953) from Halle an der Saale, who was the first to use the term "bioethics",
as early as 1926. It is a revised history of bioethics with an overview of all 22 of Jahr's known published papers. The analysis follows the diffusion after 1997 of the discovery of Fritz Jahr worldwide and
particularly the contribution of Croatian bioethicists to it.
Bd. 43, 2019, 154 S., 34,90 €, br., ISBN 978-3-643-91134-6

Iva Rinčić; Amir Muzur
Van Rensselaer Potter and His Place in the History of Bioethics
Van Rensselaer Potter (1911 – 2001), the biochemist-oncologist of University of Wisconsin-Madison,
was long been related to the invention of the term "bioethics". Even today, knowing that the German
theologian Fritz Jahr (1895 – 1953) is to be credited for this invention, Potter's ideas do not lose on
their importance, primarily for his opposition to a bioethics narrowed down onto biomedical issues.
The book represents the first monograph on Potter's life and work worldwide, telling a fascinating
story about a concerned top scientist and humanist.
Bd. 42, 2019, 126 S., 29,90 €, br., ISBN 978-3-643-91133-9

Tatjana Grützmann
Interkulturelle Kompetenz in der klinisch-ethischen Praxis
Kultursensible Ansätze zum Umgang mit interkulturellen Situationen in der Klinischen
Ethikberatung
Aufgrund von Migrationsprozessen, individuellen Lebenskonzepten und multikulturellen Behand-
lungsteams erleben Mitarbeiter im Gesundheitswesen eine zunehmende kulturelle Diversität und
damit verbunden interkulturelle Konfliktsituationen. Anhand von Fallbeispielen werden Lösungswege
aufgezeigt und praxisorientierte Techniken zum professionellen Umgang mit derartigen Situationen
im klinisch-ethischen Kontext vermittelt. Ansätze für eine kultursensible Ethikberatung, strukturelle
Maßnahmen sowie Interkulturelle Kompetenz für Klinikmitarbeiter werden thematisiert und Experten
im Rahmen von Interviews hierzu befragt.
Bd. 41, 2016, 244 S., 34,90 €, br., ISBN 978-3-643-13489-9

Hans-Martin Sass
Cultures in Bioethics
Biotopes and Bioethics are highly complex and adaptable systems of Bios. Individual bios is termi-
nal, but the stream of Bios goes on. Basic properties of Bios such as communication and cooperation,
competence and competition, contemplation and calculation, compassion and cultivation come in different shades of light and dark in individuals and species, in history and ecology. Hans-Martin Sass
discusses the territories of Bios and Bioethics, based on his involvement in decades of consulting in
academia, business and politics. Special attention is given to the vision and role of Bioethics in research and training, in religious and cultural traditions, and in the survival, happiness, and health of
corporate, social and political bodies.
Bd. 40, 2016, 260 S., 39,90 €, br., ISBN 978-3-643-90755-4

Simone Horstmann
Ethik der Normalität
Zur Evolution moralischer Semantik in der Moderne
Bd. 39, 2016, 268 S., 34,90 €, br., ISBN 978-3-643-13146-1

LIT Verlag Berlin – Münster – Wien – Zürich – London
Auslieferung Deutschland / Österreich / Schweiz: siehe Impressumsseite

Philosophie – Sprache – Literatur
Prof. Dr. Hans-Ulrich Lessing (Universität Bochum)

Ulrich Tschierske
Erotisches In-der-Welt-sein
Zwischen Körper und leiblicher Existenz
Der Autor, ehemaliger Hochschul- und Gymnasiallehrer, beschäftigt sich mit den zeitgenössischen Formen des Begehrens und der Einheit von Liebe und Tod vor dem Hintergrund der leibphilosophischen Tradition und der aktuellen Moderne. Damit sind Themen von überragender humaner Bedeutung (im Sinne Kants) angesprochen, die von der zeitgenössischen Philosophie jedoch in nahezu bestürzender Weise vernachlässigt werden.
Unter Rückgriff auf Platon, Nietzsche und Heidegger, aber auch unter Einbeziehung französischer Denkansätze (Sartre, Merleau-Ponty, Bataille, Foucault, Marion) und von Impulsen der modernen Literatur, der Musik und des Films entwickelt der Verfasser eine eigenständige und polyphone Philosophie des erotischen In-der-Welt-seins, die auch in sprachlicher Hinsicht lesenswert und überzeugend ist.
Bd. 11, 2019, 404 S., 34,90 €, br., ISBN 978-3-643-14329-7

Cornelia Eşianu
„Und so führt die Philosophie zur Poesie"
Systematische Studien zu Friedrich Schegel
Dass der heutigen Literaturwissenschaft der anthropologische wie transzendentale Akzent im Begriff der Poesie abhanden zu kommen scheint, soll weder verwundern noch alarmieren. Friedrich Schlegel bezeichnete seine Zeit als eine „entgeistete", der er vorwiegend auf den Wegen der Poesie und Philosophie und ihrer Verbindung durch das menschliche Vermögen der Einbildungskraft zu begegnen versuchte. Warum gilt die Philosophie noch immer als eine „hilfsbedürftige" Wissenschaft, die zu ihrer „Vervollkommnung" einer Ergänzung bedarf? Das Buch rekonstruiert in systematischer Weise, indem es sich sowohl in die Nähe als auch in Distanz zum theoretischen Friedrich Schlegel begibt, die Geschichte einer solchen Verbindung. Es ist jene vielversprechende Geschichte, in der sich Fantasie und Vernunft im Bewusstsein des Menschen wieder gleichermaßen einzufinden haben.
Bd. 10, 2016, 416 S., 19,90 €, br., ISBN 978-3-643-50736-5

Gaetano Chiurazzi (Ed.)
The Frontiers of the Other
Ethics and Politics of Translation
vol. 9, 2020, ca. 248 pp., ca. 29,90 €, br., ISBN-CH 978-3-643-90708-0

Miriam Rainer
Zögern / Hesitate
Versuch über das Übersetzen mit Walter Benjamin
Bd. 8, 2015, 182 S., 29,90 €, br., ISBN 978-3-643-50649-8

Ulrike Bardt
Das Selbst in Geschichten
Philosophisch-literarische Konzeptionen narrativer Identität
Bd. 7, 2020, ca. 304 S., ca. 34,90 €, br., ISBN 978-3-643-12535-4

Esther Schröter
Erzählen, (Lebens-)Geschichte und Identität im Werk Hannah Arendts
Bd. 6, 2014, 280 S., 24,90 €, br., ISBN 978-3-643-12531-6

Kevin Liggieri
Zur Domestikation des Menschen
Anthropotechnische und anthropoetische Optimierungsdiskurse
Bd. 5, 2014, 152 S., 24,90 €, br., ISBN 978-3-643-12474-6

LIT Verlag Berlin – Münster – Wien – Zürich – London
Auslieferung Deutschland / Österreich / Schweiz: siehe Impressumsseite

"Human Potentialities"
Studien zu Aldous Huxley & zeitgenössischer Kultur
Studies in Aldous Huxley & Contemporary Culture
/ edited by
Prof. Dr. Bernfried Nugel (Universität Münster) und Prof. Dr. Lothar Fietz (Universität Tübingen)

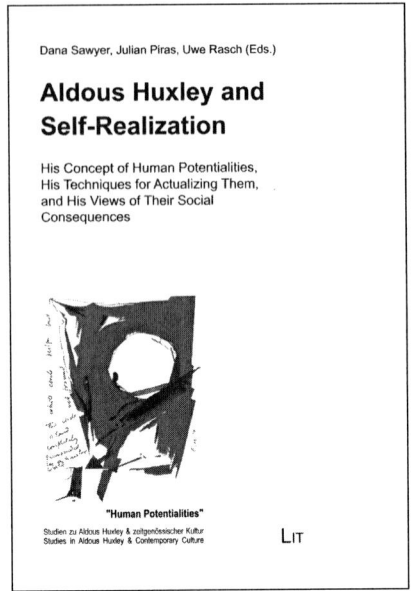

Dana Sawyer; Julian Piras; Uwe Rasch (Eds.)
Aldous Huxley ans Self-Realization
His Concept of Human Potentialities, His Techniques for Actualizing Them, and His Views

Throughout his writing career, and especially in the last thirty years of his life, Aldous Huxley exhibited a deep interest in human potentialities, which he often described as our greatest unused natural resource. The present volume is the first book to focus on this Huxleyan core concern. It is based on presentations given at the Sixth International Aldous Huxley Symposium held in 2017 at the University of Almería (Spain).

This volume collects essays by eleven scholars from eight countries that discuss Huxley's concept of human potentialities from an interdisciplinary perspective. This is another innovative feature of this book, since today Huxley is mainly remembered as a novelist, although only eleven of his fifty published works belong to that genre.

The topics of this volume span Huxley's mature philosophy, including his theories relating to the expansion of consciousness, the development of nonverbal humanities, the need to improve bio-ethics, the role of nature, the role of beliefs and prejudice, and other subjects. These essays review Huxley's various positions, shedding light on their possible significance for today. Huxley marshalled his remarkable intellect to the project of improving the human condition, and here we find an up-to-date report card of his theories and their efficacy.

Bd. 12, 2019, 270 S., 49,90 €, br., ISBN 978-3-643-91138-4

LIT Verlag Berlin – Münster – Wien – Zürich – London
Auslieferung Deutschland / Österreich / Schweiz: siehe Impressumsseite